THE OPEN
PARTNERSHIP

THE OPEN PARTNERSHIP

Equality in Running the Schools

CHARLOTTE RYAN

McGRAW-HILL BOOK COMPANY
New York   St. Louis   San Francisco

Auckland Bogota Düsseldorf Johannesburg London Madrid
Mexico Montreal New Delhi Panama Paris São Paulo Singapore
Sydney Tokyo Toronto

Library of Congress Cataloging in Publication Data

Ryan, Charlotte, date
The open partnership.
Bibliography: p.
Includes index.
1. Community and school.   I. Title.
LC215.R92   370.19'31   76-26889
ISBN 0-07-054360-7

123456789 BPBP 75432109876

This book was set in Times Roman by Creative Book Services. It
was printed and bound by Book Press. The designer was Christine
Aulicino. The editors were Nancy Frank and Cheryl Hanks. Milton
Heiberg supervised the production.

For E. F. R.

CONTENTS

PREFACE

THE IDEAS DESCRIBED HERE as an open partnership took shape over many years. When our children were first in school, we were fortunate in finding collaborative teachers, and this created expectations which later on were not always fulfilled. Subsequent years in school board membership, in legislative activity, in working with educational organizations in various offices, and in seeking more openness in local school systems all served to emphasize broad personal interaction as a key to bettering the educational process. More recently, in watching—and sometimes being caught up in—the unhappy spread of rivalries in the ''house of education'' and in watching the efforts of students to be involved in their own education and of community people to gain a voice in the education of their own children, it seemed imperative for all of us to find better ways of working together, both for fulfilling the promise we make to boys and girls and for the survival of reasonable self-governance for public education.

The concept of open partnership as such a better way grew partly out of working with numbers of people across the country who are concerned about children and about schools (one learns to prize the variety of contributions in native wisdom and knowledge from all sorts of people) and partly out of the habits of group process which become virtually second nature to long-time PTA workers.

There are many from whom I learned along the way. It was in

National PTA's organizational self-study in the mid-1960s, with the help of our consultants, Dr. Ronald Lippitt and Dr. Jean Butman of the University of Michigan, that I first began to identify specific differences between hierarchic and collaborative governance, and to see possibilities for a more collaborative structure. The concept of equal decision sharing as the basis of school-community partnership owes much to a pioneering venture of the New England Program in Teacher Education (NEPTE) whose board of directors, as member Elmer Dodge put it, has been willing to "shingle out over the fog." With NEPTE's director, Dr. Roland Goddu, and his associate, Dr. Lewis Knight, our committee searched out a handful of New England schools which met the decision-sharing criterion. At about the same time, the Manchester project fortuitously tested a number of partnership factors, including open membership and step-by-step decision making by group agreement. The resulting program grew to involve two-thirds of the students in the high school, and I believe the equal membership of students in the initial discussions contributed to a lasting school and community partnership climate, in which untoward "incidents" have not occurred for more than two years. For me the project was one of a number of satisfying experiences in working with young people. Youth contributes much to any partnership in honest appraisals and clear perspectives, and I want to include in this acknowledgement our own children, who have been among my best teachers.

There was and still is a great deal of novelty in some of these concepts; thus the invitation of Dean Dwight W. Allen to make a doctoral study at the University of Massachusetts offered a welcome opportunity to explore the validity and promise of partnership ideas. The process of developing a case for collaborative governance in a hierarchic society could not fail to require a substantial clarification of one's own values and make considerable demands on one's willingness to face difficult questions. The students I was privileged to teach raised demanding questions and contributed much from their own experience; I am grateful to them. I am deeply indebted to Dean Allen and to the interest and support of his colleagues, Professor

David W. Flight, Professor Daniel C. Jordan, and Dr. Donald T. Streets, and also to Dean Vito Perrone of the University of North Dakota.

My first intention was to publish the dissertation, but both the ideas and the available evidence continued to expand, and the outcome was that this book was written twice. During the period of preparation for final publication, it has seemed to me that the book could already be written again with new material, as so many new examples of equal and sharing relationships come to light day by day.

While the concept of open partnership has grown out of concern for better education, it is capable of other applications. Recent years have seen more and more social problems that are neglected at one level pushed up to the next level, and the next. Thus a host of matters that used to be handled by families and by towns are now decided by states, and sometimes by federal agencies. The result is loss of community. People are less able to manage their own lives and become more restless and dissatisfied. At the same time there is much waste of talent, energy, and money because responsible agencies and organizations build walls around their own jurisdictions and prerogatives. More efforts on the part of individuals or groups to work together more effectively to solve specific problems could help reverse these trends and do much to strengthen our society.

Besides the indebtedness I have described, I am grateful to many friends for help and interest. Particularly I am indebted to Roland Goddu, who read both manuscripts and whose facility for spotting obscurities was an invaluable aid, to William D. Boutwell, who gave much practical advice and generously championed these ideas, and to my family for unfailing encouragement.

THE OPEN
PARTNERSHIP

CHAPTER ONE

Introduction

THIS BOOK IS about equality. It is about shared decision making by all who are affected by or concerned in the common enterprise of education, that is, the open partnership.

If most people enjoyed doing as they are told, and if a few people were really wise enough to decide for all of us, we would be happier with our present school governance. It is a paradox of education that what is essentially a collaborative process—the process of learning and teaching—is increasingly fraught with differences and rivalries. People who should be working together are often at odds, and thus impair the learning which is their common objective.

Schools magnify an increasing dilemma of our society. Within a political framework of equal citizenship, the habits of our society are those of hierarchy: waiting for someone else to make the decisions. We may be irritated by those decisions, we may feel they were made with inadequate information and small concern for ourselves, but we are used to it. Even when hierarchic governance becomes authoritarian, whether in schools, in industry, or in government, our protests are surprisingly infrequent.

Some people are comfortable in a hierarchic niche, especially when the governance is benign, tenure is secure, and the job is right. But there are many others whose frustrations teach dogs and children to stay out of the way at the end of a day. It has become a staple of wry humor that some assembly-line auto workers take the whimsical protest of tying loose bolts to obscure parts of passing cars. In schools the persisting controversy over hair and dress codes, smoking areas, and other such minor concerns are the overt prototype of an underlying struggle for adult respect.

If the pettiness of such incidents indicates the uneasy acceptance of hierarchic governance in daily living, much more serious events show limits of tolerance: increasing resort to psychiatry by many individuals and the concerted revolts of workers, of teachers, of students, and especially of minority groups, where authoritarian practices are deeply damaging. It is not the assignment of graduated responsibilities which brings hierarchic governance into question but rather the subjection of individual lives to decisions made by other people in other interests—decisions in which individuals affected have not participated and whose interests are disregarded. People who feel disregarded and denigrated tend to draw in upon themselves, to make decisions in personal and self-centered terms, and more and more often to act out frustration in violence.

Thus it is the evil flowering in the quality of our society which most calls our governance system into question: casual crime among the young, increasing violence of ''law enforcement,'' which itself carries earmarks of revolt against court delineations of constitutional rights, sharply adversary tactics taken by some citizen advocacy groups, and the increasing hazards to bystanders.

There is a root problem in the questions, To whom am I responsible? Who are my constituents? Most teachers, when asked to whom they feel responsible, respond, ''To the principal.'' Legislators are frequently given a difficult choice between constituent interests and leadership directives. Those ambitious of leadership usually recognize that they have one constituent or set of constituents who matter: the people at the top. This intensifies competition among peers and lessens regard for clients. It is the rare leader at the top who supports objective attitudes among subordinates. Rather, the hierarchic system encourages subjective, self-serving attitudes. The advancement process thus tends to weed out client-oriented officers and to develop a more rigid organization.

In recent years the conflicting currents of societal change have brought more pressures on schools than the dominant hierarchic governance could manage. The dismaying spread of rivalries in the "house of education" has made difficult the natural interest of parents in their children's education, frequently placed students and teachers in adversary positions, and brought legislatures into more and more regulation of schools. The public in general is far less certain of the quality of our schools now than just a few short years ago, and it is considerably less willing to make the necessary investments. It seems imperative for us to find better ways of working together, both for fulfilling the promise we make to boys and girls for a society worth living in, and, more immediately, for public education and the survival of reasonable self-governance.

In this painful situation current proposals for the reform of school governance call upon most of if not all of the methods that people have tried in the cycles of change throughout history:

1. *Revolution*. Destroy, rebuild from a new beginning. Deschool society. Revolutions characteristically take on a life of their own, even in microcosm, with consequences well beyond the imaginings of their progenitors. But some people think seriously in this vein.

2. *Change in the balance of power*. Most proposals of this sort would shift decisive power from professional authority to lay groups other than school boards. Forced change lasts just as long as coercion is possible, however, for coercion does not persuade. Moreover, coercion is destructive of human relationships. The history of nations is interwoven with old enmities and their consequences; so is that of many small societies such as schools and organizations.

3. *Adversary action*. Usually focused on immediate goals, adversary action utilizes available resources to bring about specific change. Some groups "demand" rather than "propose" or "recommend" and support demands with threats. Some protest demonstrations and many political strategies fall into this category. Adversary action is sometimes successful, but it carries the risk of

inspiring not merely equal but greater reaction, to the point that one could almost rewrite the Newtonian law. The price for immediate success may be a greater loss later on.

4. *Advocacy*. Probably most of us who seek change settle for persuasive and persistent statements of our beliefs and wishes. We lobby. We educate public opinion. We organize support. In current practice, however, advocacy is institutionalized: in education it consists of organized public intervention on behalf of students against schools, which are seen as institutions concerned primarily for themselves.

5. *Negotiation*. An associate of Martin Luther King told Mary McGrory that the same day Bull Connor put police dogs and fire-hoses to the protest marchers in Birmingham, Dr. King sent his representative to talk with people from the Birmingham Board of Trade. "I don't care how much we marched in the streets," this associate said, "how much we boycotted, how powerful our political moves, without a quiet reasonableness, there would have been no progress."[1]

There is no substitute for quiet negotiation behind the scenes, no substitute for the exchange of opposing views and the step-by-step accommodation which can bring opponents to acceptable terms. Nevertheless, many of us approve of negotiations for others but are unwilling to engage in negotiations in our own affairs. Sitting across the table in negotiation denotes equality. Unwillingness to accept employees in equal responsibility for their own welfare brought years of sometimes bloody strife in industry. Today industrial managers generally value the help of union organizations, while in education the controversy over "professional negotiations" is only partway along a similar path. Those on one side are saying, "But professional people are different from industry!" and those on the other are responding, "But we still want equal status." Because professional negotiations are not yet accepted as appropriate, and their scope is

---

[1] *Mary McGrory, The Washington Star Syndicate, Boston Globe*, June 14, 1975.

not yet mutually defined, they have in many cases taken on an adversary character.

6. *Collaboration* or *partnership*. Negotiation alone is not enough in that important interests are sometimes lost in the bargaining and, further, in that many creative possibilities of shared thinking may be left untapped. Collaboration is by definition reciprocal in its concern for common goals. Groups or individuals with common interests in the success of an enterprise can gain more for themselves and for the enterprise by sharing a concern for each other's interests and seeking solutions which satisfy the interests of all parties involved.

In contrast to each of the foregoing methods, partnership is a situation in which "everybody wins." To take an adversary or advocacy position is to be content with a "win-lose" situation, although, if advocacy should develop through a policy of involvement and shared information, advocates could find themselves in the collaborative situation of "win-win."

The nub of the collaborative process is that decision making is shared by all who are concerned or affected in any instance. The attitudinal barriers to such sharing can be substantial, both in those who are used to making all the decisions and in those who are used to being excluded: both doubt the propriety of change. But once these barriers are overcome, the rewards are great. People join more willingly and purposefully in work when they have participated in developing the goals. Moreover, if individuals have been enabled to combine their own goals with those of the common enterprise, participation also leads to individual growth and satisfaction.

Schools whose teachers, students, parents, administrators, and interested public share in educational decisions are today making substantial growth in meeting their educational objectives. In spite of conventional wisdom, school boards and their administrators *can* share decision making without creating difficulties for implementation. Students *can* join in determining their own governance with substantial gains in educational achievement. For lay groups, collaborative initiatives *can* be more effective than adversary action for bringing about change.

This book offers partnership methods as techniques which provide an effective choice both for making present governance structure livable and for developmental change. Because so many adversary situations grow out of hierarchic or line-of-command organizational patterns, out of strict professional role assignments, and out of assumed territorial responsibility, however, the concept is explored and techniques suggested from the perspective of each of the protagonists in the educational scene: the school board members, the administrators, the teachers, the students, and interested laymen. Whether the reader explores each of these interest areas in turn, or follows the story of partnership theory in Chapter Two by moving directly to the practical steps and techniques in Chapter Eight, the writer hopes the reader will be encouraged to take advantage of the almost daily opportunities in which the validity of these principles may be tested.

Partnership Schools

IN ONE NEW ENGLAND TOWN a few parents and other interested citizens raised questions for several years about the lack of diversity in the college-oriented high school curriculum, without visible effect. The PTA brought in outside speakers to describe career education and open-campus programs. A curriculum committee excited mild interest with recommendations about student choice. When the state department of education issued guidelines for advisory committees on open-campus programs in career education, guidelines which gave such committees unusual powers of recommendation, a small group of parents and teachers approached the superintendent.

The group requested permission to create an open-invitation committee, instead of the announced small group of appointments, to study possibilities and develop a proposal. With some hesitation, permission was granted. In early May 1971 a newspaper story announced a meeting date and invited all persons who might be interested. Forty-three citizens, students, administrators, faculty, school committee members, and interested townspeople attended the first meeting. Of these perhaps a dozen had been invited or appointed by the skeptical superintendent. As the committee organized and worked over the summer, and its activities were publicized, the number of active members grew to eighty-nine.

They came for various reasons, some because of their interest in the concept of off-campus curriculum, some because, as one parent put it, "I want the best educational facilities possible in Manchester, but I am also fairly conservative and wanted to make sure that no hasty or ill-advised 'curriculum revolution' would occur."[1] Some businessmen came to be assured that students would not be "downtown doing nothing." All of these joined in broad exploration of a community-based curriculum for some seven months before coming to a firm consensus on recommendations which were approved and implemented.

At its first meeting the group organized itself into subcommittees to visit other schools, canvass community resources, and conduct school surveys. All meetings were open and their proceedings well publicized. During the discussions sharp differences in educational goals sometimes appeared and were accepted. The group used the practical method of writing joint policy statements in successive approximations to set goals and work through a variety of problems. They agreed to set aside differences of views that did not pertain to off-campus curriculum. Both the subcommittees and the group as a whole concerned themselves to arrive at accommodations only as required by the common purpose. There were some complaints as new people joined the group and under the open agenda policy ground already covered was covered again in new discussions. The outcome, however, was that the recommendations which went to the school committee (school board) in December were so well explored and so broadly accepted that the committee responded with an immediate and unanimous vote of approval.

The advisory committee was then concerned that the program be implemented immediately, fearing loss of momentum should the budgetary process delay a beginning until September. Fortunately the committee secured a small federal grant to enable the program to be installed with the new term in January. In June the first evaluation found that a number of able students who had been close to dropping out had taken a new liking for school. Some had identified lasting

[1]Charlotte Ryan, *Open Partnership: The Manchester Expanded Curriculum Project*, New England Resource Center in Occupational Education, Newton, Mass., 1972, p. 3.

career interests. Some teachers had begun to work together who had not previously done so. Community people had gained in the process a better understanding of the dynamics of school staff situations; many school faculty felt the value of community alliances; and both groups gained new appreciation of students as colleagues.

In succeeding years the advisory committee continued its supervision of the program, monitored the budget allowance, participated in annual evaluations, and publicized the continuing growth of the program. At the end of its third year two-thirds of the high school students were involved in off-campus activities under individual contracts carefully integrated with their educational programs, and it was felt that the new "Expanded Curriculum" was satisfactorily integrated into the high school program.

In the process a variety of new leadership had emerged among teachers, students, and other citizens who had not previously taken such roles. People had learned to work together in a colleagueship which spread into other areas. There was a perceptible easing of tension between parents and teachers in discussing education. Students were fully accepted thereafter in school-related interest groups. While the administration did not fully accept the values of open membership, because the next advisory group was entirely appointed, it did recognize the values of numbers and of diversity. Thereafter ad hoc advisory committees of thirty or forty members became accepted procedure. At the same time the open-membership PTA tripled its numbers and broadened its activities.

This enterprise was illustrative of several partnership components: open membership, multiple leadership, open agenda, and shared decisions taken step by step. The process was slow in the beginning; decisions came more quickly as facts were gathered and people came to trust each other. In its self-evaluation late in the school year, the committee agreed that the openness of committee organization was a major factor in the success of the program. Openness made it possible to draw concerns to the surface early in the discussions, concerns that might otherwise have seriously diminished support and made cooperation more difficult. Another constructive factor was the core of hard workers, people who either were or made themselves knowledgeable in education. Yet here too the practice of openness made these workers available. Such a group is likely to be available in any community, and with proper encouragement will come forward as needed. Most of all, perhaps, the incident shows how partnership is learned; patience, perseverance, and a common concern for the students developed a colleagueship in which mutual trust made decision making objective and comfortable.

IN ANOTHER STATE, the new school staff of a newly consolidated rural school wished to utilize community resources in the curriculum and discovered that success required earning the colleagueship of community people. They encountered the obstacle that citizens who are used to traditional schools are inclined to suspect frequent trips outside of school as wasteful of time and money, saying, "They ought to be in school."

In this school, a general lack of interest in reading among their students led the faculty to develop a carefully planned curriculum around visits to sites of industry, commerce, and natural phenomena within a wide area. They called it "Horizons Unlimited."

"Our children weren't reading, weren't interested in reading, because they weren't interested in much of anything," explained the principal, Evelyn P. Burnham.

> When we tried to expand their background of knowledge about the real world, they began to be interested in reading, and that's where it started. Then we thought it really had more credence as a general philosophy of education for the whole school than just for reading. Everything should have some application for the child in his general development; and in tying his learning to reality, we should use the resources we have, which are in the community as well as in the school.[2]

---

[2]Colebrook Elementary School, Connecticut; data from personal visit and monthly staff reports, New England Program in Teacher Education (NEPTE), monitoring small grants in supply of building school-community partnerships, 1973–1974.

Initially a reading grant was secured to fund the program. The staff asked parents to serve as drivers, and organized a sequence of visits to see many examples of the world at work. Children were taken in small groups, and site exploration was integrated with the children's work in school. The students reacted with enthusiasm and began to stop as they entered school in the morning to check the week's schedule posted by the door.

Involving the community in the classroom was an equal objective; parents coming to the school were delighted with the openness of their welcome, and accepted invitations to stay and help with classes. Other community people were invited to come into classes to describe their own jobs and various interests as part of Horizons Unlimited. The teachers recounted as a special success story that one sixth grader, assigned as teaching assistant to the second grade, confided her teaching difficulties to her father, who gave her some effective advice. It was the first time he had taken an interest in the school.

As the grant funds were expended, however, and continuation of the plan depended on acceptance into the following year's budget, the staff were worried. The skepticism of the superintendent had not been dissipated by such incidents as finding the entire school out watching the workmen install new portable classrooms. The principal said, "They would all have been looking out the window anyway, and we might as well have made a learning experience out of it."

Since the community had not been involved in developing the new curriculum in the first place, success in keeping the program depended on persuading the community of its value to the children. The annual town meeting was held in the school, and the staff took pains to explain what was going on in the school through displays and posters. They placed other displays in the post office, and persuaded civic groups to hear their story. By the middle of the second year they could show definite improvement in the children's reading levels, and had the support of established relationships with many families. There was, moreover, much evidence of a warm and creative learning climate in the school. When the budget was finally decided late in May, the staff had won the support of both school board and superintendent. They had built collaboration through involvement and their scrupulous accounting for their program.

IN 1972 the New England Program in Teacher Education endeavored to identify "partnership schools" in New England by offering small grants to groups which met the criteria of joint decision making. Of ninety-two applicants only three schools offered plans developed with equal participation by school and community groups. The three schools are described in the following pages.

Two private-school teachers came from New York to Vermont in 1960, and in 1965 the couple moved to an isolated one-room school. Both Claire and Albert (Mac) Olglsby had open-education experience; since there was only one job, Claire became the teacher and her husband became her part-time aide. Well aware that successful introduction of other than traditional methods necessitated community support, these teachers began by searching out community talent to share with the students. People were sometimes surprised to find themselves teaching, and teaching with confidence; but gradually there were enthusiastic classes in sewing, baking, cooking, tumbling, art, music, play writing, foreign languages, photography, shop, and drawing, as well as the basic subjects, in this one-room elementary school. The school became a community learning center, hosting holiday parties, square dancing, ski trips, and ice-skating. Parents remodeled and painted the schoolhouse. The students created a school-community museum, and in summer the school became a movie house. Gradually the curriculum included trips to plays and museums and a regular sequence of visits to the places where each parent worked. One of these places was the State House at Montpelier, where the legislator parent introduced the students to the State General Assembly. Discussions of community activities and issues became part of social studies classes. Students began working with adults in the community in agriculture, in a carefully designed ecology curriculum, and in developing recreational resources.

A high degree of partnership was achieved in efforts stretching over several years, involving the entire neighborhood and other schools in the district. A parent-teacher advisory group determines priority for new programs. Observers are impressed that the smallest student is treated as much as an individual as any adult. The Vermont Department of Education made a training film of the school, and as a national resource in teacher education in the open-classroom concept, the school has had hundreds of visitors. One rural community in Washington State sent its teacher to learn about the only one-room school its school authorities could identify which involved parents in this manner.[3]

Partnerships can come out of sharp differences in views, even out of controversy. One experimental inner-city school, which was originally established by parents, became enmeshed in conflict over questions of control among parents, teachers, and administration, and sought partnership as a way to survival.

Parents started Highland Park Free School in 1966 as an alternative preschool program for thirty children and added grades as the children grew older. By 1972 the school had 220 students aged four to fourteen divided into three teaching units with individualized, nongraded instruction. Parents raised the necessary funds, selected staff, and dominated its decision making. For some time certified staff necessarily came from outside the immediate community which the school served, and this was a source of misunderstandings. Nevertheless, staff and parents shared the commitment that the school should serve the total community, which comprised a largely low-income population, and that the school's curriculum should be identified with the community's culture and its survival needs.

In order to assure community influence in instruction, the parent board provided each classroom with a certified teacher and a preprofessional "community teacher." The two teachers planned together, implemented plans together, and day after day met after school to evaluate what they did that day and plan for the next day. The

[3]Westminster West, Vermont; data from staff reports, New England Program in Teacher Education, 1972–1974; cf. "Claire Oglesby's 'Magic' Works," *The Common*, March 1973, and Frank W. Morgan, Jr., "Vermont's Community-involved 'Open' School," *American Education, June 1973.*

community teachers organized community participation in school life, and were at the same time enrolled in teacher preparation through the Career Opportunities Program.

Scarce funding, however, not only left staff with noninstructional problems such as a failing heating system, but also curtailed resources available to solve instructional problems. The faculty could not give their students learning experiences in a wide variety of actual community activities—economic, cultural, and political—for lack of ability to command resources beyond the immediate neighborhood.

It was in the process of seeking funds for this purpose, and of planning the enlargement of curriculum, that joint committees of parents and teachers were created for the first time. This moved their attention away from concerns of power and control toward program concerns, and helped both parents and teachers to a better understanding of students and of each other. As a small grant eased the situation slightly, parents and teachers learned to work together in finding outside teaching resources, arranging cooperation with other institutions, and designing and building classroom materials and equipment. At the same time the administrators and teachers began to redefine their roles. Teachers began working together to initiate new projects, evaluate materials, and coordinate resource programs. Administrative responsibilities were restructured. As James D. Cooper, master teacher, reported, "The hassles were lessened and the energies of the Master Teacher redirected through the establishment of an administrative team."

About three years later the school did close for lack of sufficient funds. In the meantime, however, the grant had enabled the school to explore ways in which the parent board and the teachers could share rather than worry about control of the educational process. In retrospect, staff and community members felt they had achieved a valuable understanding of the partnership idea.[4]

---

[4]Highland Park Free School, Boston; data from reports of school staff and of staff of the New England Program in Teacher Education, 1972–1975.

In an inner-city public school, professionals and non-professionals, veterans and newcomers alike speak of "the partnership" with warmth and pride. This seven-year history began with a joint parent-teacher appeal to the city school board to transfer an unsatisfactory principal. At the same time the group asked and received permission to choose a new principal. Their successful choice began a lasting collaboration which came to involve all the staff and the larger part of the community served by the school.

The new principal, Charles Senteio, brought a federally funded Teacher Corps team to the school, one of whose members was a paraprofessional from the community. In order to involve more of the community, the team offered summer reading and science programs for both grade-school children and the high-school-age Neighborhood Youth Corps. At the same time, looking toward the fall, they canvassed the homes for classroom resources and volunteer aides.

Did the parents take their ideas seriously? "Yes, because we had a strong PTA," replied Mrs. Daniels, the one-time paraprofessional who became one of the school's best teachers.[5] Teachers and parents alike speak warmly of how the parents learned that for the first time they were really welcome in the school. They were encouraged to work in their children's classrooms (often with preschoolers in tow) listening to reading or numbers and giving other help. The PTA appears to have become identified with the partnership ("The PTA *is* the partnership!") early in the process. A PTA chairman, sometimes a teacher and sometimes a parent, has coordinated the volunteer program under a steering committee. The resource file built up by a succession of such chairmen includes both paraprofessional and parent aides and instructional resources from the community and the city. The steering committee of thirty members makes decisions about school and community-shared activities, with a

[5]Barbour Elementary School, Hartford, Connecticut; data from personal visits, school and partnership documents, and monthly staff reports, New England Program in Teacher Education, 1972–1975.

coordinating committee of five members. These and other task committees meet on different Saturdays, with all meetings open to interested community members and school staff.

In subsequent expansion of their efforts, the group formed an
educational partnership with the Connecticut General Insurance
Company, planned new recreational facilities with the city park department, and, with a taste of their collective power, secured a traffic
light in front of the school after an angry bout with City Hall. ("It
was exciting being hauled off in the paddy wagon," said one young
teacher.)

Within the school the partnership obtained a federally funded
Follow Through program for the primary grades, planned and held a
series of in-service training programs, developed a fifth-grade open
classroom, and established a school lunch program, besides construct-
ing classroom materials, holding a weekly ballet class for boys and
girls, and organizing field trips. Management of these various activities and the procedures involved have developed what amounts to
in-service training for citizens in management techniques, as well as
training for paraprofessionals in the classroom, and have resulted in
actual jobs for low-income residents.

The principal chosen in 1968, and his successor, Virgil
Franklin, were in turn hired away to broader opportunities. In the
summer of 1973 the partnership interviewed, screened, and selected
a new principal for the third time, Fred Morris. After six months in
his new school he commented, "Nobody can say he didn't have a
chance to get involved, because the partnership opens the door to
everybody. It brings everybody together. Here, everybody's involved; that is the major difference [from his previous schools]."

The school has not been without its problems, particularly when
teacher turnover has broken up effective teaching teams or when a
new principal has found decision sharing more demanding than he
expected. Some task chairmen have been more efficient than others.
Some leaders have been more effective in sharing decision making
than others.

On the other hand, the partnership has been recognized as an evolving process. There have been periodic exercises for evaluating the partnership process, both for the legitimacy of its directions and the self-development of the participants. The partnership idea has undoubtedly created a stronger linkage of the people involved. The parents queried all say that it feels much more comfortable talking to and asking questions of teachers. Many parents have long since taken the initiative to go into the schools and offer help to teachers as well as ask questions. Teachers have seen that different skills and approaches in the classroom are desirable, and have learned to value parent as well as paraprofessional help in instruction. The idea of a community educating itself has emerged and approaches reality.

In the spring of 1975 the school board proposed to close the school as part of a retrenchment program to meet declining enrollments. The partnership effectively protested not only with general meetings but also with documentation of the space needed to house the innovative curriculum that had been developed in the school, and the inability of the proposed substitute space to accommodate the same program. In some admiration the school board accepted the protest and the school remains open.

THE PARTNERSHIP METHOD

The prime characteristic common to all of these schools is that diverse groups of people worked together for a common objective.

A partnership implies equality. It implies the sharing of concerns, of risks, and of benefits. In a school-community partnership parents, teachers, students, and other citizens bring together their concerns and their particular expertise to address given needs of children or of schools in colleagueship. Few of us know individually what can or should be done in a situation of any complexity, but if we come together we can talk through a problem and arrive at a better solution than any of us could have discovered separately. Thus, building the partnership depends on people working together as individuals, successfully. The process in which a group of individuals produces substantive results and lasting agreements depends on respect between members so that everybody feels free to put his or her best effort into the common enterprise, and therefore all interested segments of the population are encouraged to join.

Anyone can begin a partnership by saying, in effect: "We have a common concern; can we talk about it?" For the school administrator, it may be the simple decision to let others help, to set aside the feeling that one must as a responsible administrator make all final decisions. The administrator cannot impose a partnership; by its nature a partnership is voluntary. He can only invite faculty and staff or other interested citizens to share consideration of a problem with him, on the clear assumption that they will also share in the decision making.

Conversely, the invitation may be initiated by teachers, students, or lay community members who are not ordinarily involved in significant decisions. A certain political skill is helpful in making the invitation. The request of one person is less likely to be effective than that of a small group; a visit of more than three or four, however, may appear to be a confrontation unless its good nature is very clear. Nevertheless, the simple request, "May we talk about it?" is hard to refuse.

In any case, it may be that the invitation is not accepted immediately by all who are concerned. The partnership begins with those who are willing, and the invitation to all others to join at any time remains open and warm. The partnership may be formally organized in various ways; it may comprise a group interested in one segment of the school operation or the whole "school community": that is, not only school board, administration, faculty, and students, but also parents and other citizens interested in education, tax burden, or other aspects of school operation. The objective in any case is to involve all who are concerned in any common problem in finding a satisfactory solution.

The degree of formal organization required in any instance may depend upon the complexity of the problem, the numbers involved, and the range of sophistication in the group. Of basic importance are effective fact-finding procedures and sharing of all information with the total group. These procedures should include sharing of research tasks among teams with both lay and professional members. Such sharing not only develops broader information but also helps to eliminate "caste lines" between lay and professional members.

Likert has summarized the differences between solutions reached independently, by compromise, or by a collaborative approach:

1. Independent approach to achieving a common solution:

a. MY facts	analyzed and interpreted in terms of MY experience	yields	MY solution, which I think is good and to which I am committed.
b. YOUR facts	analyzed and interpreted in terms of YOUR experience	yields	YOUR solution which YOU think is good and to which YOU are committed.

If one wins, the other is not motivated to help with the implementation. If there is compromise, both may be half-hearted.

2. Coordinated fact-gathering approach:

Same facts	analyzed and interpreted by each person separately in terms of his experience	yields several solutions, depending on number of persons and range of previous experience. But because of use of same facts, solutions are likely to be less diverse than in process 1, above.	One solution achieved by conflict or compromise and with corresponding motivational consequences as stated in process 1. But conflict and compromise are apt to be less bitter than in process 1 because solutions are less diverse due to same facts.

3. Approach based on coordinated fact-gathering and group decision:

Same facts	analyzed and interpreted by group in terms of experience which is shared in the discussion process. This leads to less diverse experience being focused on decision-making processes.	Wide variety of decisions examined but narrowed to one solution	yields solution based on experience drawn on in the sifting and integrating done in seeking the solution. Solution accepted by all as THEIR solution.	Excellent solution, with each person highly motivated to carry it out well.

Source: Rensis Likert, *New Patterns of Management*, McGraw-Hill, New York, 1961, pp. 216–217.

Some basic skills are involved in building a partnership: patience in hearing what a colleague feels in addition to what he seems to be saying; willingness to begin "where people are" and patience to find out where that is; willingness to explore the issues raised; learning how to be both honest and lucid in expressing one's views. The attitude is, "I'll level with you on what I really think, but I'll wait to hear what you think, and maybe I'll change my mind. Anyway, we'll try to get together, because we think we have common goals."

Willingness to look for solutions in a colleague's interest builds trust; simple discussion around a table by representatives intent on their own interests, on the other hand, builds into either stalemate or bargaining. Lasting agreements are not arrived at through compromise made simply to avoid conflict, or by mechanisms such as majority vote or trade-off. In fact, one of the commonest misconceptions about collaboration is that it is equivalent to compromise. The difference between the solution which is compromise and the solution which is the fruit of collaboration is that in compromise each "side" gives up something, and ordinarily ends with less than it had, or desires to have, in order to arrive at an acceptable solution. Collaboration, on the other hand, leads to joint efforts resulting in better and generally more acceptable solutions for all than any participant can devise separately. It is therefore to be avoided that some win and some lose, because with sufficient effort a solution can be found in which everybody wins.

Once the discussion is opened, a number of other problems on that same question are also legitimate agenda, and it is necessary to allow time for an exchange of concerns and a setting of priorities. Continuing involvement of responsible authorities throughout the process is important, because it is not within the partnership concept to delegate decision making, reserving the possibility of exerting a veto later on. This does not mean that the physical presence of the administrator or anyone else may be required at all times; the presence of any individual's view may be felt, and the effort may be organized so that those who may be concerned with a particular point are involved or represented in the progress toward solutions.

Disagreements are helpful in suggesting a wide range of alternative solutions and in providing needed information. Agreements too easily reached may not sustain the impact of reality because real situations have not been adequately studied. Final agreements should be acceptable to all members as fully explored and as most satisfactory of available solutions.

Leadership in discussion takes many forms: asking pertinent questions to advance the discussion, introducing new ideas, clarifying issues, testing ideas against data, elaborating ideas that others have suggested, summarizing what has been said or what still needs to be explored. Equally important is leadership which encourages and offers warmth to other members, or offers alternative solutions. Another kind of leadership visibly resists or tempers the occasional member who "pulls rank," magnifies unimportant details to exclude an important aspect of an issue, or expresses hostility.

Openness has a way of obviating the role conflicts which are common in schools. In sharing the work of solving significant problems, individuals are able to emerge with all their various strengths and leave their roles aside. This is especially facilitated in talking through the amazing vocabulary differences which exist in any group in order to establish an understanding of each other's concerns. Addressing real concerns with other people is opening one's self to change as well as others; thus, opening partnership is also initiating personal growth.

Finally, patience at the beginning of any partnership effort is essential to arriving at a productive conclusion, whether a short- or long-term effort is intended, whether a single objective is involved, or whether the effort is to introduce a partnership climate throughout a school and its community. It takes time for people to know one another and learn how to work together easily. Indeed, time pressures are probably the major obstacle to any partnership; attention to organizing the work to avoid unnecessary time restrictions will be rewarding.

A successful partnership effort, however small, will have good effect well beyond the program area involved in creating a favorable climate for further efforts. The habits of collaboration will carry into other activities. Thus, unlike adversary efforts in which immediate change is the objective, the long-range effects of partnership go well beyond success in the immediate venture.

THE QUESTION OF POWER

Probably the major challenge to partnership ideas derives from the undeniable attraction of power. Because legal responsibility is equated with authority and control, decision making is regarded as a perquisite of power or as a managed outcome of power conflict. Differing interests therefore find themselves directed into some sort of adversary action.

In some organizations and societies office and responsibility do follow power, but in school governance legal responsibility remains relatively fixed, and power does not. In any society, any situation, however, power is not an attribute of any person or group, but is a relationship between some person or group with power and others who accept that power. Thus power is a deceptive goal, for it "generates from the controlled."[6] What the "controlled" have granted, even by acquiescence, they can also recover. It may be a simple refusal to continue acceptance of a specific control, as when Rosa Parks stayed in place on an Alabama bus. It may be a slow-down operation on an assembly line, or the ignoring of a central office directive in a public school.

In other words, no leader, authority, or controller can successfully direct those whose performance he would control or for whose performance he is responsible unless the latter accept his direction. In school governance, where legal responsibility is fixed, the unwillingness of people to accept direction may lead to difficulties in operation and perhaps to diminished performance. Teacher militancy, student unrest, and an increase in audible parent dissatisfaction in recent years document the dilemma. All these groups clearly object to being left out of decisions which concern them. Logically, therefore, the best way to reduce the vulnerability of leadership and increase its value is to share decision making with those involved and concerned.

This concept requires a certain sophistication of leadership, however, and many school administrators and board members view with misgiving the notion of sharing the controls they now hold in school governance. Collaborative governance has been given a great deal more study in relation to industrial management than to education. Research inquiring into industrial management characterized by high productivity found that the motivation of workers is closely bound into the compatibility of their goals and the goals of the organization. If the goals have been imposed, or if there is conflict between the objectives of the organization and the needs and interests of the workers, there is a lack of trust and confidence. If, on the other hand, the objectives of the organization have been developed out of the findings, the efforts, the technological growth, or

---

[6]Donald J. McCarty and Charles E. Ramsey, *The School Managers: Power and Conflict in American Public Education*, Greenwood Publishing Corporation, Westport, Conn., 1971, p. 10.

changing conditions experienced by the workers, then there is high motivation to produce at maximum levels.[7]

To school administrators, however, the idea of involving in a decision those who are concerned or affected by that decision generally seems radical. What happens to legal responsibility? Under present legal assignments of authority, participation in decision making easily takes place in the preparatory stages. While decision sharing may entail giving up present convenience for a farther goal, it requires no change in legal responsibility. A great many decisions are substantively delegated by school boards and by school administrators at the present time—decisions for which they hold legal responsibility. Substantive decision making can be shared on matters of joint concern between administrators and teachers, or between teachers and students, and the task responsibilities of each role still apply. That is, the teacher is still a teacher, the superintendent is still superintendent, and so on. But each can contribute usefully to an assessment of problems and to possible solutions, both from a task point of view and from his or her individual knowledge and experience.

More than administrators and teachers are to be involved, however. Actual responsibilities for the welfare of the school are broader than the legal responsibilities. Both parents and nonparent taxpayers are deeply concerned with various aspects of progress and accomplishment. The effectiveness of any school or school system depends in many ways upon variables in the community which cannot be controlled by the school, such as willingness to maintain fiscal support, competing costs of municipal services, rapid changes in population, or emotion-producing crises involving school personnel. All these problems can be addressed in fragmentary fashion, and commonly are. If, on the other hand, people are more broadly involved, not only are broader solutions made possible, but significant additional benefits appear. The process which involves all commu-

[7]Rensis Likert, *New Patterns of Management*, McGraw-Hill, New York, 1961; Robert R. Blake and Jane Srygley Mouton, *The Managerial Grid*, Gulf, Houston, 1964.

nity groups will enlist support well beyond the particular matters which may be the subject of immediate discussions and will thus tend to offset unexpected untoward influences, for human beings respond as positively to being involved in responsibility as they do negatively to being excluded from decision making. The carry-over is that, both within the school and in school-community relations, the continued sharing of information and exchange of views which is essential to decision making creates over a period of time among the people involved a climate of trust in which they resolve differences more easily and work together more creatively and productively.

There is much evidence that the sound growth of public schools is closely related to the acceptance by school boards and school administrators of a more modern management role. Because education is a collaborative process, it is best served by collaborative governance.

In summary, just as Likert and others have urged upon industrial management the participatory methods of achieving higher industrial productivity in a time of economic challenge, so it is important for school management, for the sake of good education, to count those who are involved in the educational enterprise as allies and colleagues, rather than employees, clients, or frequent adversaries. The authority for operating schools is unchanged. Rather, the managers share the fact-finding, the reality testing, and the onus of their decisions. They profit by the surfacing and the resolving of unsuspected differences. They are supported in implementation of difficult decisions, and can count on a more productive implementation because of the wider interest generated in the decision-making process.

THE OBJECTIVE OF CHANGE

If those who manage the schools may be reluctant to accept collaboration, so, very often, are those who are lower in the hierarchic scale, who feel controlled or excluded. Others, too, feel the attraction of power. It is ironic, perhaps, that so many reformers who would secure participation in decision making for laymen, students, or teachers are seeking "power for the powerless." It seems that we tend to behave as others have behaved to us, and many people have learned to want power from those who have exerted power over them. Such groups commonly mobilize for adversary action.

Especially when advocacy of change is rejected, the advocates may fall into an adversary position. The most tempting situations for taking adversary action arise from frustrations in which there seems no opening for collaborative intervention. A common situation is the apparent blockage of community groups by school administrators in their advocacy of some educational alternative. What seem to be evasive answers, broken appointments, cordial but meaningless hearings, and similar devices are all part of the experience of many such groups. It matters little whether the blockage, if blockage it is, protects policies already decided upon or really amounts only to self-protection against pressures beyond the administrator's personal endurance. It is hard for such groups to resist taking adversary action.

Part of the picture, too, is that many a school administrator has set out to attract "community participation" and been frustrated by unreliable attendance at well-intended meetings, by differing agenda, and by various communication barriers. It is easy in such cases for the administrator to fall back upon appointment of "reliable" people to advisory committees with specified tasks.

In other situations school boards who are contemplating change may invite the views of various groups but play one against the other. This places the representatives of the several groups in competition with one another, defending different proposals instead of working for a common objective. Forcing people into adversary positions in this manner makes it difficult for those who are concerned to develop collaboration with one another, as well as to involve the school board in the collaboration.

Nevertheless, there are a number of reasons why it is advisable for individuals or groups who seek change to initiate a collaborative arrangement.

In the first place, adversary action tends to bring about reaction;

rather than being "equal and opposite action," moreover, it often seems that action brings a greater reaction, and the end result is often far from that which was intended. Conflict is seldom considered legitimate in a hierarchic community, and those who have raised an issue which is considered to have caused conflict are resented and likely to see their opponents multiply. Collaborative action, on the other hand, can ameliorate dominant control by involving other interests of the community.

In the second place, the process of change in schools is notoriously slow, not because proposals are lacking in merit, or because school people are uninterested, but because quite generally "change agents have underestimated the complexity of the organization they dealt with. Often they have viewed the problem as mainly that of convincing professionals that some new innovative scheme or program will result in increased learning for pupils."[8]

What is neglected is the effect upon others of change introduced at any point in the total fabric: people easily feel threatened by the suggestion of unexpected change because it may necessitate undesired change in their own lives. These feelings, together with the inertia of individual burdens, soon blunt change efforts. As the experience of the identified partnership schools indicates, one does not successfully "sell" change, or impose it. Change comes about by interaction, involving and affecting the individual or group acting as change agent as much as any others.

In summary, the change agent must involve all who may be affected by change in determining what that change shall be. This insight is helpful in developing the patience and tolerance required in building a partnership. Beyond this, however, it is useful for each of the partner groups to know something of the general thinking, the problems, and the hopes of other colleagues. To assist in this understanding is the intent of the next few chapters.

---

[8]Richard C. Williams, Charles C. Wall, W. Michael Martin, and Arthur Berchin, *Effecting Organizational Renewal in Schools: A Social Systems Perspective* McGraw-Hill, New York, 1974, p. 125.

CHAPTER THREE

School Boards
and the Partnership Idea

MANY ARE THE SCHOOL BOARD MEMBERS who seek election in order
to bring about changes in their schools, only to find after election that
it is not nearly so simple to bring about change as it seemed from
outside. They may have intended to introduce educational innovation
or return to "basic" curriculum, to cut school costs or see that more
money is spent; whatever their hopes for change, they generally
encounter a situation already complicated with protocols and coun-
terinfluences. At any one time a school board may be subject to both
internal and external pressures for such changes as improving vocational education, cutting the instructional budget, adding new opponents to the football schedule, and upgrading the reading scores.
Gradually new members also find that their powers may be limited
by available funds, by local politics, by state and federal legislation,
by the prerogatives of state and federal agencies, by involvement in
religious, racial, or economic antagonisms, and not least by the
traditional separation of policy and administrative powers and protocol requirements for staff recommendations.

The most baffling part of the situation for our hypothetical new
board members, however, and the most significant part, is that
school governance and operation are what Allen has called a "seam-

less fabric''; [1] change at any one point involves consequent problems all along the line. That is, if the recently elected member or anyone else should persuade the board to adopt a program, and the superintendent is so instructed, implementation still requires change in procedures by a number of other persons who may or may not be willing to accept change.

The paradox between such realities and their understanding of school boards' legal powers tends to leave board members somewhat bewildered. School board members generally express frustration with the relatively small portion of control they feel they can actually exert over their school system. While their legal responsibilities cover the total operation of the schools, their actual room for decision is commonly set at 5 to 10 percent of the school budget, and about 5 percent of curriculum. That is, state salary minimum levels or state salary schedules, plus existing staff levels and annual professional negotiations, together with various mandated services, determine the greater part of the conventional school budget. The greater part of curriculum may be mandated by the state agency or appear glued into place by college entrance requirements or local custom. Changes are likely to require agreement from teaching staff, from parents, and perhaps from state agencies.

In addition, the board has little direct control over the quality of learning that actually takes place. Student achievement depends not only on available curriculum but also on such school-related intangibles as teacher-student collaboration and the prevailing climate of expectations. [2] School boards frequently do not understand how their

[1] Dwight W. Allen, talk given to Joint Conference of Massachusetts Association of School Committees and Massachusetts Association of School Superintendents, Oct. 15, 1970.

[2] cf. Gunars Reimanis, *Teaching Effectiveness and the Interaction between Teaching Methods, Student and Teacher Characteristics*, Corning Community College, Corning, N.Y., 1972; George Domino, *Interactive Effects of Achievement Orientation and Teaching Style in Academic Achievement*, American College Testing Program, Iowa City, Iowa, December 1970; Robert G. Scanlon, *Factors Associated with a Program for Encouraging Self-Initiated Activities by Fifth and Sixth Grade Students in a Selected Elementary School Emphasizing Individualized Instruction*, University of Pittsburgh, Pittsburgh, 1966.

influence can be exerted to improve student learning. More often than not, despite the talents and dedication of thousands of able school board members, the outcome is frustrating. In 1970 Ben Brodinsky described his own Connecticut school board to a meeting of the American Association of School Administrators (AASA) as a typical situation.

> Most of our actions around the board table are defensive, restrictive, argumentative, punitive, trivial, or controlling of some minor administrative item. . . . Yet meetings . . . last well into the night. And after each meeting I am usually overtaken by a disturbing question: what have we accomplished for the good of education, for the development of our children?[3]

Five years later National School Boards Association (NSBA) officers reported to their annual convention that the American school board is on trial on charges of irrelevance, trivia-clogged agenda, needless controversies, and the "insiders' club."[4] As one studies the situation, however, such charges appear only symptomatic of deeper problems: (1) alienation from the general public who are school board constituents, (2) contentious relationships with superintendents and other professional staff, and (3) generally inadequate policy management.

For more than a decade critics have raised a cry that "school boards are obsolete," while the defense for lay control of education is hampered by declining public confidence in its elected representatives. A Gallup poll conducted for NSBA recorded a widespread ignorance of board functions, negative reactions to such problems as rising school costs and various kinds of disruptions, and resulting alienation.[5] All reports indicate that public concern with education is increasing, but this does not necessarily mean better school board-community communications. Indeed, in issues on which school boards are dependent upon community understanding of school

[3]*The School Board Meeting*, National School Public Relations Association, Arlington, Va., 1970, p. 46.

[4]*Education U.S.A.*, Apr. 28, 1975, p. 201.

[5]*The People Look at Their School Boards*, National School Boards Association, Evanston, Ill., 1975.

needs, such as the voting of tax levies for school support and bond issues for school construction, the record of the past ten years is dismal.

The contentious relationships between superintendents and school boards of most large cities[6] have helped to drain public confidence. Moreover, such "bickering" between school board members as was cited by a Chicago superintendent as reason for his resignation[7] may be as great an obstacle to good management as the more publicized bitterness between boards and teachers' organizations. While the situations of city school systems are more visible in the national media, similar relationships are commonly reported in many local newspapers and even in school board journals.[8]

Controversial board relationships may stem from a number of factors. Some boards are representative of segments of the total community and tend to be competitive for the interests they represent. Some members have trouble in distinguishing between personal and group authority. Board members may be dissatisfied with information and either may seek their own data or challenge the superintendent; some boards retreat to nonessential agenda. Because superintendents generally prepare agenda and initiate proposals, some board members feel that this gives superintendents a means of dominating meetings. Some board members differ with their superintendents on educational values and objectives. Dependence on majority vote leaves many issues unresolved. Despite the value conventionally placed on lay leadership and lay control of education, the educational expert is frequently accorded greater deference; school board members therefore tend to an uncomfortable feeling that theirs is but hollow authority and trust between board and superintendent breaks down.[9]

[6]*Time*, July 28, 1975, p. 39.

[7]*New York Times*, July 5, 1975.

[8]Cf. Margaret Jacques, "The Divided Board—Is It as It Should Be?" *MASC Journal*, Massachusetts Association of School Committees, June 1975, pp. 3–5.

[9]Cf. L. Harmon Zeigler and M. Kent Jennings, with G. Wayne Peak, *Governing American Schools: Political Interaction in Local School Districts*, Duxbury Press, North Scituate, Mass. Copyright © Wadsworth Publishing Company, Belmont, Calif. Donald J. McCarty and Charles E. Ramsey, *The School Managers: Power and*

All this conflict militates against good policy management. A study of Massachusetts school committees (school boards) led Cook[10] to observe that almost all committee meeting time was taken up with the details of budgets and teacher negotiations; that, while both these concerns would argue a need for strategic planning, what he found was "a virtual absence of strategic planning in the intermediate term sense," that is, how to get a school system from where it is to where it seeks to be. Cook finds poor management of school committee time affects total school management. "Viewing the system as a whole," he continues, "one would have to conclude that probably less than one-tenth of one percent of the people, time, or money involved in public education is devoted to how the system as a whole should and can be changed."

One might suppose that the functions of a school board would parallel those of a board of directors in industry. In business and industry, however, directors and trustees usually have the same professional background as the officers of their companies. Vocabularies are similar, and therefore communication tends to be clear. School boards, on the other hand, are generally nonprofessional in education, and administrators try hard to keep it so. When educators are occasionally elected to school boards, administrators tend to feel a competitive element in the deliberations. As a result communication problems may increase.

The crux of the problem is that planning, development, and management skills are by nature collaborative, and where communication is constantly at risk, collaboration is difficult indeed. The reason for lay governance of education is the unique obligation of schools to society for preparing its next generation. The emphasis on the division between lay and professional competence effectively hampers the interchange which can sharpen professional perspectives of student and community needs. Moreover, there are values in

Conflict in American Public Education, Greenwood Publishing Corporation, Westport, Conn., 1971.

[10]Paul W. Cook, Jr., *Modernizing School Governance for Educational Equality and Diversity*, Massachusetts Advisory Council on Education, Boston 1972, pp. 41–43.

exchange between colleagues of different backgrounds which go beyond immediate questions and are largely lost in present school board practices. None of us ever explains himself in any case without understanding one's own job better. When deliberations are shared between colleagues of different expertise, both lay and professional members are enriched in perspective and competence; the result is that management policies are considerably more likely to be responsive and stable.

BEHIND SCHOOL BOARD ORIENTATION

The influences in school board orientation which have tended to develop adversary rather than collaborative roles in board-administrator-community relationships have been consistent policy choices of both professional and school board organizations over many years. Orientation has centered, first, on the dimensions of school boards' legal powers and, secondly, on drawing distinctions between the board's policy-making role and the superintendent's administrative role. In practice, the distinction between policy and administration is frequently blurred by board members' sometime interests in school operations, but the principle leads to the board's drawing an employer-employee relationship when it chooses to do so, and to the superintendent's dealing with the board on a political basis. Both inclinations tend to accentuate adversary feelings.

The emphasis on the boards' power of final decision, rather than on the deliberative process leading to appropriate decisions, tends to deprive the process of substance; the decision making is likely to lean on short-term considerations rather than educational philosophy. A board is dependent on the superintendent's choice of supporting information, and a board member's inquiry for other data tends to take on an adversary cast. Yet it is hard for a board member to learn about schools without a degree of participation of some sort. Even in the development of written board policies, by NSBA guidelines,[11] a

[11]*MASC Journal*, Massachusetts Association of School Committees, Boston, June 1975, pp. 31–36.

board is expected to depend on the administrative staff or, alternatively, on an outside consultant for the actual writing of policies; the board's role is simply to discuss and reject or accept the statements, without enjoying the creative exercise of actually putting together the ideas and definitions. In result, board policies tend to grow from administrative rather than from board thinking, and may be a continuing source of differences.

The same emphasis on decision-making powers leads to alienation from the community. Observation of board members and board operations suggests that the very consciousness of their decision-making powers inhibits the development of collaborative skills. In any question of educational change, board members tend to reiterate their possession of these powers and thus isolate themselves from the kinds of community involvement in educational affairs that would bring about collaboration. The professional emphasis on separating lay and professional concerns in education further adds to the isolation of school boards in the community by identifying the boards with the school system, but on the other side the same convention isolates the boards from the schools.

In recent years school board members have flocked to conferences and conventions in ever-increasing numbers to seek answers to their problems. A myriad of programs have been given over to questions of school finance, professional negotiations, and various educational innovations. Educators advise that conflict is a normal situation to be handled by giving latitude to the superintendent; seldom is it discussed in terms of the improving skills and leadership of board members. The public is discussed as neutral, supportive, or adversary, seldom collaborative. In one widely reported conference, H. Thomas James[12] spoke of "sharing different points of view" between boards and superintendents but concluded that "the strategy of the successful board must be 'to free the rational part of each board

[12]*School Boards in an Era of Conflict*, *Education U.S.A.*, Special Report, Highlights of the Cubberly Conference, Stanford University, Stanford, Calif., July 26–28, National School Public Relations Association, Washington, D.C., 1966, pp. 2–3.

member's mind from the irrational at the time when decisions must be made.''' One or two speakers at the same conference referred to the need for respect among board members, and ''consensus rather than the conviction of a close majority'' as the best basis for decisions. But if the specific skills of goal setting, planning, and collaborative decision making were addressed at any point, it was not reported.

Rubin[13] said that the single most important problem of school boards was to distinguish between the responsibilities of boards and the responsibilities of their designated superintendents. There are gray areas, inevitably overlapping roles of adviser and consultant, in which reciprocal respect is essential. Without it, the board should hire a new superintendent or the community elect a new school board. But in the end Rubin called upon state legislatures rather than collaborative procedures between board and superintendent to define the superintendent's responsibilities and impose their execution.

Minar[14] used case studies to show that ''popular participation in school affairs is a mixed blessing.'' Of ''two school systems with high-status and low-election participation, one maintained a stable position'' without public interest, few observers at board meetings, and minimal communication with the public; board meetings were short and ''the superintendent in a strong position . . . [for] policy initiative.'' The other district came under constant scrutiny and pressure, with every board meeting drawing a crowd. Under this stress the board showed signs of conflict: its meetings became long, formal, and tense, and much business was done by preagreement. ''The superintendent's policy initiative is still broad, but the board tends to chip away at it, often on unimportant matters.'' Minar's case studies appear to have dealt typically with boards which separated themselves from the public they served. The ''good board,'' Minar said, ''provides a good administrator with 'running room.' It would not impose community demands on school policy, but instead would

[13]Max J. Rubin, in ibid., p. 13.
[14]David W. Minar, in ibid., pp. 15–16.

urge the superintendent to take chances and assure him it would take the heat if public opposition developed."

This widely held and conventional view of board-super-intendent-community relations suggests clearly that the school board's chief responsibility to the community is to support the superintendent, because he or she would know what is best for the community's schools. It tends to create a sense of separation between board and community, as opposed to a sense of board responsiveness to community views.

The difference is accentuated by accepted board status as a quasi-judicial body. Procedures manuals for school board meetings generally stress open meetings and the privilege of citizen presenta-tions. Some writers, such as Harold Pierson,[15] stress provision of full and adequate information to the public, as well as the importance of listening to citizen views through media, meetings, complaints, and direct contact. Pierson urges a careful program of providing school information through mass media, school publications, in-volvement of the public in school affairs, and encouragement of direct contact with citizens by all school personnel. He urges that equal effort be made to secure citizen feedback through school-community partnerships or advisory committees, a planned program of parent-teacher conferences, analysis of questions and complaints coming to the school office or put to school personnel, monitoring of circulating gossip, and use of public opinion polls. The net of these findings must be utilized both in the information program and in board deliberations. "Public disagreement with the board," writes Pierson, "is a clear signal for the board to review its own decisions in the light of public discontent."[16]

Few school boards develop two-way communication as care-fully as Pierson prescribes it; if they did, it would help to alleviate the implications of sitting in judgment which tend to cast thinking and process into an adversary rather than a collaborative mold. Under the

[15]H. L. Pierson, *Shaping the Schools: A Guide to Boardmanship*, Harold L. Pierson, New Hampton, N.H., 1973.
    [16]Ibid., pp. 93–98.

best circumstances, school boards hear presentations by members of the public; they do not engage in an exchange of views. Thus board members may or may not have fully understood a presentation and its implications, and it may be questioned whether decisions made in later and substantially private sessions of the board satisfactorily relate to the presentation.

In addition, it is commonly observed that most boards like to avoid dissension where possible. If some members are reluctant to discuss the subject matter of a presentation, development of significant points is thereby avoided. When citizens raise questions about the need for an exchange of views, the common response is that there is no legal requirement for discussion. For that matter, there is no legal requirement even to hear presentations. Only the presiding officer may give permission to speak; this power can be used to maintain an orderly proceeding or, equally well, to prevent citizen comment. An argument is often capped by the reminder that the power of decision lies with the board in any case.

Citizens who appear before school boards therefore sometimes feel that their participation is more cosmetic than functional. The resulting frustrations among citizens tend to lead to the adversary activities on the part of citizens of which school boards sometimes complain. As one PTA president exclaimed in some exasperation, "When can we stop being nice?" The question was not rhetorical. Under the circumstances the answer was, "You don't stop being nice, and you don't stop."

SEEDS OF PARTNERSHIP

A few students have explored the possibilities of shared decision making between school boards and other constituents of their school systems. Among these Bendiner[17] quotes Cyril O. Houle in support of a collaborative relationship:

[17]Robert Bendiner, *The Politics of Schools*, Harper & Row, New York, 1969, p. 34.

Both board and executive have complete responsibility and therefore the dividing line of authority can never be drawn. Only when the attempt to divide the two is abandoned and they are seen as inseparable partners can progress be made.

Houle would extend this joint use of power all the way, "including planning, organizing, staffing, directing, reporting and budgeting." Lay and professional partners, in other words, would join their experience, knowledge, and expertise in behalf of the schools. Bendiner himself finds this advice out of date, because the "power to be divided is so diluted . . . that this relationship is no longer the central issue in the governing of our schools."

The issue of shared decision making persists, nevertheless, and becomes the focus of a detailed report of interviews with approximately five hundred members of eighty-two representative school boards across the country.[18] The study tried to identify how school board decisions are made. It documents a broad spectrum of superintendent-board-community relationships ranging between two extremes: board deference to professional direction on one hand and subordination of the superintendent's recommendations to the board's view of community values on the other. While the former relationship tends to predominate in cities and the latter in small towns, there is no pattern: complexities abound. Despite growing state and federal involvement, the findings place immediate control over school policies at the district level; but, the study found, control is not in the boards. They "have been effectively insulated from the voting public . . . and increasingly dependent on superintendents for information on which to base decisions."[19]

The study reports increasing public concern with the schools and the "suspicion" that "the isolation of schools is being reduced." It concludes "that any reform movement must deal simultaneously with the relationship between the representatives and the public and the interaction of the board and the superintendent." The authors explore the question of competence for educational decision making and end their report with these words:

[18]Zeigler and Jennings, op. cit.
[19]Ibid., p. xi.

In spite of the obvious perils, political decisions are—as long as we remain committed to democracy—logically superior to technical decisions. . . . Boards are the mechanisms whereby schools can be made more responsive to their constituencies. Whatever the perils that more responsive schools may bring, the costs of insulation from the community are greater.[20]

If school boards are the key to responsive schools, they clearly cannot do the job alone. Indeed, their isolation has been their undoing. They need interaction both with public constituents and with their administrators on an equal collaborative basis. Collaboration can only be offered and invited, however, not demanded. Boards can of their own volition become more responsive to the community. The needed interaction with administrators will come about only as educators begin to regard the contributions of laymen to educational solutions as different from and yet as useful as their own. Without this change, board responsiveness to the community remains at risk of an adversary relationship with the professional staff.

Howe has urged educators to change their attitudes toward laymen.[21] Not only should they try to improve communication but involve laymen "to put other kinds of professionalism to work for the schools." He warned that unless the people believe in and support programs for change, education cannot move ahead—a truism that is politically sound but short of a partnership concept. School boards will not break loose of their isolation until both they and their executives can separate leadership from legal authority, recognize legal authority as a role assignment, and see leadership as susceptible to being shared, not only between board and superintendent as Houle suggests, but between board and other concerned citizens.

INTRODUCING PARTNERSHIP

Brodinsky continued the remarks quoted earlier (p. 30) by wondering if his board could not serve as a "public court of educational relations" once a month:

[20]Ibid., pp. 252–254.
[21]Harold Howe II, in *School Boards in an Era of Conflict*, p. 21.

In such a public court of educational relations, the feeling would not be one of the employer versus employees, of taxpayers versus public spenders, of rule makers versus those who have to obey the rules. Its mood and temper would be one of explaining, proposing, questioning, groping, exploring, and sympathetic listening.

To such a public court, students would come, at first, perhaps with shouts and demands—later with their opinions, their questions, their needs, and possibly, too, with reasoned proposals and imaginative suggestions. . . . Let's open our doors and agendas for this purpose.[22]

Here would be the exchange of differing views which is one mark of collaboration. Such discussions the faculty and parents of the "partnership schools" commonly have. Although a judicial concept is implied in using the term "court of educational relations," the proposal is nonjudicial and participatory. It is not clear, however, how the discussions are to relate to school board decision making. People are attracted to partnership discussions because they are assured of a voice in the outcome. Membership in partnership discussions is diverse and open, but above all it is equal. People who meet in partnership are searching together for appropriate and acceptable means to solve a common problem.

Limited examples of this sort of discussion are not unknown. One very successful instance has been taking place in Montpelier, Vermont, for the past several years. It happened that the teachers' association—not the school board—initiated the exchange by inviting the board to an informal discussion, with social amenities, of any and all matters of interest not included in professional negotiations. The first meeting was so successful that it has been continued twice a year and has become a fixture. Both groups comment that it has developed good relations within the school.

Any board would gain wisdom in its deliberations if it were able to attract the kind of discussion Brodinsky described. It must be recognized, however, that it is not easy to persuade people to open

---

[22]*The School Board Meeting*, p. 47.

themselves to the extended discussion that might be required or to make the effort of collecting data and analyzing their own views sufficiently for productive discussion unless they see a useful purpose. If teachers, parents, students, and other citizens felt that doing so would give them voice in decisions on their own interests, the likelihood is that they would come. In meeting this expectation, of course, the board would be opening itself to equality, but this is a hurdle not unlike that which boards have already taken in conforming to open-meeting laws.

Let us spell out, for a moment, the possible differences in procedure between the usual board meeting and a board-conducted "partnership" discussion. In the first place, partnership discussions are targeted; therefore a board would initiate discussions when a particular problem excited interest, and would issue an open invitation to the people concerned. Secondly, partnership discussions turn early to exploration of relevant values; Brodinsky's "shaking dreams loose" becomes purposeful in developing educational goals. A very tangible change in common board procedure would be the process of "successive approximations" in which tentative decision statements are proposed, tested, and revised. Those concerned would be present and involved in the development, testing, and formulation of policy decisions. When implications can thus be fully explored, the procedure becomes very different from the common practice of "backing into policy change" with offhand or piecemeal decisions. In matters of curriculum, for instance, by broader involvement of community and faculty, the board can bring about integrated curriculum development instead of fitting together the fragments of special-interest programs which various groups insist upon.

A board member sometimes says about the partnership idea, "We tried having discussion and then 'they' didn't like what we did. Aren't we, in opening up our discussions, taking a risk of developing more opposition?"

Two factors are significant in avoiding such an outcome. First, satisfactory solutions are seldom if ever reached in one or two meetings with a problem of any magnitude. If there are deadlines to be met, a board can organize its schedule to deal with them without impairing the discussions or the decision-making process. The second factor arises from the actual legal authority of the board, which remains unchanged. Immediate action by the board is still available at need, but it is an alternative that should be kept for emergency. If members are inclined to keep their prerogatives in mind, rather than the problems in hand, they may not open themselves to consideration of all data, or of the evolving ideas in the partnership discussions. The thinking in the back of board members' minds, if this occurs, may still be in terms of "we" and "they" rather than in terms of shared concern and shared responsibility. In consequence, the faculty and other citizens who have been involved may sense the impairment of the partnership and withdraw from the joint endeavor. If partnership discussions are pursued, on the other hand, small and temporary impasses in understanding may still occur, and discussions come to stopping points. The solution is to recess and meet again, to prevent the stopping points from turning into conflict.

It will be recalled that a basic concept in the partnership idea is that leadership is not limited to the professional or elected leadership roles. Rather, at any given time any individual may be offering the kind of leadership needed at that time: new ideas, relevant facts, analysis, summary, encouragement, or whatever. This "alternate leadership" inevitably occurs in an open partnership, simply because of the wide distribution of talent among any group of interested people. That this may be a confident expectation should lighten the burden of those school board members who may feel the weight of decisions most heavily. The larger problems, whether they emerge in board meetings or are raised elsewhere, are profitably put into the partnership process for solution. Since a variety of matters may well be under consideration at any one time, the process could well be organized in a pyramidal structure of discussions. Separate groups would discuss separate issues; those involved in each discussion would be those concerned with the issue.

The safeguards to the board's trusteeship in this process lie in what goes on before the recommendations are written for the board's final decision: in the thoroughness with which the discussion is conducted, the involvement of those concerned, the agreement on the dimensions of the problem and on the goals for solutions, the exploration of the underlying realities, and the diligence in searching for solutions. Frequently the agreement on the dimensions and nature of the problem is the lengthiest and most significant part of the whole procedure.

The partnership process might appear to take longer than discussion by the small group of school board members, but when decision is reached, the board is free of concern about possible adverse reaction in staff or community. It can be relatively confident of effective implementation. Problems are far less likely to return for repeated attention when satisfactory solutions are found than when given what amounts to one-sided consideration. Further, when larger problems are satisfactorily solved, a substantial number of related smaller questions are not only more easily solved, but often can be referred to implementation levels.

Probably the most important outcome of the open partnership is that school governance comes to be based on goals and leadership. As was indicated in the beginning of this chapter, school board members cannot by any means impose quality of learning "from the top," but they can develop it by modeling collaboration within the schools. When board members regard the superintendent as a public employee, not as their employee, and themselves as trustees rather than as authority figures, board-superintendent relations more easily take on aspects of colleagueship. Despite the admonitions of the textbooks, in a partnership situation the several members of the group do not forget their roles. When the members have confidence in one another, and have made decisions together which they all find acceptable, there is no question who is charged with implementation. The board members have no inclination to interfere with administration when they have confidence in what they have done together. Neither do they take on separately tasks which belong to the group when they have come to trust the group's decision-making process.

When school board members have greater confidence in the dynamics of interest and competence within the schools and less in imposition of controls, when boards are willing to involve people all along the line in determining their roles and the curriculum they teach, school faculties have greater confidence in developing systems of accounting and evaluation for self-improvement. Under such circumstances there are real possibilities of ameliorating the power conflicts in professional negotiations, which will be discussed in a later chapter. Instead of dropping into parity of conflict, boards can best preserve their prerogatives by building mutual respect and parity of influence. School budget making, so often the center of community demands for school control, benefits by agreed-upon plans and is released from many uncertainties in priorities and citizen support.

As to the quality of student learning, what school boards cannot impose they can help to bring about. The collaborative model influences relationships in schools and classrooms, with a positive effect on the quality of student learning. Finally, as board members may well most appreciate, all the trial and effort which partnership building involves will serve to establish their leadership in the community as clearly fulfilling their public responsibility.

CHAPTER FOUR

The School Administrator in a School-Community Partnership

OF ALL THE GODS, Janus must have a special meaning for superintendents. Leader and gatekeeper, agent and guardian, the superintendent plays a dual role, with one face to the school board and the other to the system. It is at the same time the most influential, the most exposed, and the most vulnerable role in education.

The other side of the board-superintendent syndrome which we discussed in the previous chapter is that, countrywide, superintendents in increasing numbers charge that school boards are making their jobs impossible by wanting to make the decisions, and as a result superintendents "are not being allowed to manage the schools." In a typical case, it is reported of a superintendent that "the board tied his hands, went over his head, demoralized the staff."[1] City controversies are headlined, but the same conflicts appear in systems of all sizes. Both boards and superintendents feel the other group is seeking total power.[2] In a concentration of pressures—fiscal, societal, and political—such controversies have erupted into public view fairly recently, but they have been growing

[1]David Nyhan, Globe Washington Bureau, *Boston Globe*, Aug. 10, 1975.
[2]*Education U.S.A.*, Mar. 10, 1975, p. 159.

[45]

for a long time. The conflict between a board's legal powers and the superintendent's managerial prerogatives approaches an impasse. In many cases this results in resignations or dismissals; other systems make do with patchwork arrangements. Average tenure becomes shorter every year.

The year that an unusual number of school superintendents in Massachusetts lost their jobs a Boston newspaper ran the headline, "Running schools not so super in Massachusetts." At about the same time the president of the state association wrote to his colleagues:

> More and more in recent years it has been brought home to the practicing superintendent that he operates in a very lonely environment. With the legislature, the parents, the general public, the state department of education, and local school committeemen all attempting to do our job for us, we are constantly in need of professional organizational clout in order to maintain our position and stature as individuals.[3]

Organizations can be helpful in that the respective officer groups and staffs of school board and school administrator associations consult with one another and can ameliorate some situations to a degree. Nevertheless the problem is essentially local. The superintendent's job under present school governance is not easily bolstered by organizational "clout." Superintendents have to do their own bargaining as individuals. Some appeal can be and is made to legislatures for job protection, but job tenure in a difficult working climate is scant comfort.

The third party to school governance is the community. Community interest in school affairs is always present and increasing numbers of citizens prefer to be participants rather than spectators. Most superintendents, however, regard public involvement as "attempting to do our job for us," if not actual interference. They turn to the community for money, but no oftener than school boards do they accept any significant help in school operation. Where excep-

[3]*Newsletter*, Massachusetts Association of School Superintendents, Boston, August 1973.

tions have occurred, and superintendents have been interested in community alliance for better schools, either they had the support of their school boards or they encountered the boards' sharp resistance, according to whether or not the boards saw the possibility of a competing relationship. In most cases, however, the absence of public participation tends to narrow the field of active concern to the board and its professional staff. Whether the relationship between these two groups is productive or otherwise has a strong bearing on the quality of the schools.

THE FABRIC OF SCHOOL MANAGEMENT

In the "seamless fabric" of education the attitudes and activities of any individuals or groups affect many others for good or ill. There is substantial evidence that boards and superintendents who develop partnership relations are likely to maintain successful school systems. Some superintendents are sufficiently convinced of the efficacy of collaborative methods, are skilled enough, and perhaps are blessed with responsive board members, so that they can develop a partnership which avoids the too-easy answer of majority rule, and learns to organize its business within long-term planning. They bring outside pressures into manageable perspective and even utilize them as sources of energy.

There have been outstanding instances of such collaboration, many of which undoubtedly go unnoticed. The superintendent of White Plains, New York, credited that community's successful experience as one of the first northern cities to integrate its schools to board-staff-community collaboration. When the schools in Shrewsbury, Massachusetts, adopted a flexible schedule of four days a week with student options for day or evening classes, and a career opportunity program in the community, the proposals came from various sources in the school committee, the administration, faculty, and community. All shared in the planning, and each typically credited the others with the program's success.[4]

[4]*The Shrewsbury Plan*, Shrewsbury Public Schools, Shrewsbury, Mass., 1973.

In both these instances people in different roles worked together objectively for an identified goal. When common goals are lacking, on the other hand, all participants tend to fall back into the accustomed "pecking order" competition of hierarchic governance.

For instance, the superintendent is more than manager of the school system and executive of the school board; in most communities that officer is also known as its educational leader. Behind the scenes, many a superintendent has felt the anomaly of the title as the school board reminds its executive that theirs is the legal power and the superintendent is strictly their employee. In such uncomfortable situations the existence of common objectives is doubtful. The question of handling information, so often the focus of power and controversy, presents the superintendent with a dilemma. Will the board give appropriate time and thought to full information in discussing major problems? Boards sometimes make decisions in a closed circle which excludes the superintendent even though that officer is sitting at the same table with them. This can force the superintendent into offering selected data which will fit the probable time allowance, or into making unilateral decisions about matters which the board has neglected, when the interests of students appear to be at stake. Still other decisions may be left to chance.

A divided board and poor working relationships at board level are commonly reflected in the problems of the school system. One school committee was sharply divided for more than ten years; the voting majority shifted with each election. According to its chairman, the group spent little time on "education," but reserved to itself all control over negotiations. At one time reluctance to "bargain in good faith" with the teachers' association led to a court order to resume bargaining, and eventually to a strike. In another instance, division in a city school committee delayed court-ordered integration for several years, impeding federal aid and creating other administrative difficulties.

Divisions within a board and divisions between board and superintendent create tensions among faculty and other staff. School governance is largely hierarchic; that is, the superintendent directs and supervises school activities through some structure of assigned responsibilities under policies theoretically determined by a lay board. His authority may or may not be adequate to the task. As theorists put it, "The superintendent has authority only when his subordinates permit their behavior to be guided by his decision without independently examining the merits of that decision."[5]

The superintendent's own plans and the clarity of his guidance are subject to the decisions of the school board. If the relationship is difficult, the superintendent may tend to create pressures on staff to avoid any "troublesome" activities. Community people desirous of innovations in their schools are sometimes unaware that resistance to new ideas among school staff or tensions in home-school relations may be symptomatic of pressures from higher levels. Harold Howe once made a characterization that came to be widely quoted: "The professional, left unchecked, is liable to become a dictator; a school superintendent is no more exempt from becoming a hometown Hitler than the most pompous and arrogant Babbitt who ever headed a school board."[6]Howe was discussing the traditional division of responsibility for schools between layman and educator, and the need for the balance of lay control. Whether or not a board can deal adequately with a rigid authoritarian may be debatable, but there is at least a possibility that authoritarian behavior is encouraged by an arbitrary school board. A suggestive incident occurred in a teachers' conference some years ago when the writer was asked to role-play a principal interviewing a concerned parent, and rather unconsciously modeled an elementary school principal known in childhood. At the end of the skit one of the audience exclaimed, "That principal is afraid of her school committee!" It was a new thought at the time, that our stern martinet might have been more defensive than hostile.

Pressures upon administrators to see that their schools run

[5]Roald F. Campbell, Luvern L. Cunningham, and Roderick F. McPhee, *The Organization and Control of American Schools*, Charles E. Merrill Books, Inc., Columbus, Ohio, 1965, p. 218.

[6]*School Boards in an Era of Conflict, Education U.S.A.* Special Report, Highlights of the Cubberly Conference, Stanford University, Stanford, Calif., July 26–28, National School Public Relations Association, Washington, D.C., 1966, p. 21.

smoothly are commonly translated into numerous regulations within the school itself. Where regulations and interests of students or teachers conflict, there is usually one answer: "It's the rule, you know." One is reminded of John Gardner's observation that the truly modern dictator achieves domination through people, not in spite of them; that many threats to individual freedom stem not from any political circumstance but from proper procedure.[7]

Bel Kaufman told her lecture audiences that after *Up the Down Staircase*[8] was published, she had letters from all over the country, from both urban and nonurban areas, saying, in effect, "You wrote about my school." Her stories of exasperating and incongruous regulations and their consequences are not yet outdated. Most school people can cite examples. A teacher is commonly transferred according to central-office determination of organizational need rather than personal preference. Team-teaching organization may be imposed without consultation, sometimes even without orientation. Students are assigned according to classroom count considerably more often than for compatibility with teaching style. Sometimes the administrator is "regretful of the necessity of these actions but sees no choice." If teachers or students respond negatively, or even passively, they may be blamed for lack of responsibility. One hears the echo of an old complaint in industry: "Why aren't people more productive? We pay good salaries, maintain good working conditions, give good fringe benefits and steady employment. Why do they do only as much as they have to?"

Recurring crises in schools have raised questions about the adequacy of school governance, especially as disruption increases even to the emergence of actual crime among students. Nevertheless almost every professional influence reinforces the habit and feeling for the necessity of control. It is increasingly clear that the vulnerability of the school administrator is directly related to insistence upon control and unwillingness to share responsibility.

[7]John W. Gardner, *Self-Renewal*, Harper & Row, New York, 1963, p. 56.
[8]Bel Kaufman, *Up the Down Staircase*, Prentice-Hall, Englewood Cliffs, N.J., 1964.

THEORIES OF SCHOOL MANAGEMENT

A decidedly expansive view of the superintendent's role appeared in the 1956 AASA Yearbook. These pages draw a picture of the superintendent as a wise and sympathetic leader; possessed of good judgment, a fine sense of values, sound knowledge of the community and its needs, the know-how to bring about teamwork, the ability to work with community leaders as well as others in all walks of life, and more than a passing knowledge of literature, art, music, history, economics, sociology, psychology, physics, biology, chemistry, and mathematics; having a good grasp of the social and economic forces that are sweeping America and the world, an educational philosophy that meets the requirements of this complex society, and a familiarity with current instructional thinking, business management, accounting, insurance, school architecture, public relations, and organization.[9]

There are and have been superintendents like this—the "compleat" person, virtually a Renaissance person—but even two decades ago school administration demanded both less and more than this. The concept lingers, in a nostalgic sort of way, and is part of the anomaly that is creating so much controversy in school governance. That is, the task of being an educational leader is added to that of dealing with a basic conflict in administrative training: a doctrine of administrative control versus the necessity of giving the individuals who make up the system enough satisfaction to behave efficiently. If there were some sort of convocation of all those who are currently speaking and writing about school administration, there might be an agreement that administration mainly seeks qualities of leadership. There is by no means agreement, however, on the degree to which an administrator should exert control of the instructional and support systems, on the one hand, or on the other, how far leadership may be identified with the coordinating skill to bring people together in pursuit of common goals. If we are to judge from the published

---

[9]*School Board-Superintendent Relationships*, American Association of School Administrators, Washington, D.C., 1956, p. 59 ff.

controversies between boards, superintendents, teachers, and some segments of the interested public, the objective seems to be control. The following discussion is a good example of conventional theory:

> Perhaps the whole concept of hierarchy is perceived as contrary to our traditional value of egalitarianism. We like to think that every man is equal to every other man. At the very least, we are confused about the matter. On the one hand we seek for our organization people who will be strong leaders, and on the other hand we attempt to limit and circumscribe such leadership as soon as it is attempted. Perhaps each of us, subconsciously, to be sure, would like to see members of the administrative hierarchy be vigorous in the decision-making of the organization as long as the decisions were consonant with our own desires. . . . When he [the administrator] behaves contrary to expectations he may easily be perceived as exercising too much power. . . .
> The principal of a school, for instance . . . is expected to implement certain policy decisions made at the level of the central office and communicated to him. . . . [M]embers of his own staff will expect him to implement policies and procedures which have grown out of staff discussion. In both cases he is to carry out organizational imperatives, not his own personal wishes. . . .
> There are those who would strip organizations of such office, who would dispense with hierarchy altogether. Were this done two alternatives seem to be available. The first is administration through group process perhaps actually exercised by one or more committees. Our experience with this procedure suggests that committees may be fully as arbitrary as a single administrator. . . . The second alternative is one of complete anarchy: each member of the organization doing as he wishes to do. . . . We have to reject these alternatives and conclude that hierarchy seems to be with us. Our task is to make it work as well as possible.[10]

The "confusion" as the writers call it is well illustrated here: if policies which have grown out of staff discussion should conflict with central office decisions, the principal has a problem. Can a reader doubt where the principal's allegiance is expected to lie?

---

[10]Campbell, Cunningham, and McPhee, op. cit., p. 234.

Again, in the process of "making hierarchy work as well as possible," Campbell and his associates recognize that "conflicts between the role expectations of an organization and the personal need-dispositions of the organization constitute alienating forces." They suggest that "to counter these alienating forces are integrating forces in the form of goals and values."[11]

Undoubtedly the most cohesive force in educational governance is an underlying, if not always apparent, concern for children and young people. Dissident forces can confuse and dampen but not eliminate this motivation. Where managers can harness human motivation to a given task, governance is clearly more effective than with reliance on direction alone. There remains a distinction, however, between utilizing staff motivation as a means of advancing administrative objectives and the determination of objectives through shared decision making, which are then implemented through assigned responsibilities. The difference lies not only in management's concepts of human motivation but also in management's views of the value of staff contribution to shared objectives.

It is essential that the differences between these theories be clearly distinguished. As a method of governance, hierarchy is older than the pyramids: executive manager at the top, with tasks delegated and assigned to individuals along the line of command, down to the groups and individuals responsible for production. Everybody has his or her place, with known tasks and established relationships. Since long before the pyramids were built, managers have assumed that material rewards are necessary for securing performance, because the average human being is understood to have an inherent dislike of work and to avoid it if he can. Where material rewards have not been enough to meet managerial objectives, managers have resorted to control, coercion, and threat of punishment. These measures have been and still are justified on the basis that, as is still widely believed, the average human being prefers to be directed and wants security above everything else.

Assuming the need for security to be an adequate motivation, a manager may seek to assure employee performance by means of:

[11]Ibid., p. 246.

1. Direction through control of jobs: i.e., "Do as I say, or else. . . . " This frequently leads to frustration and militance.

2. Provision of benefits, commonly termed "paternalism." The resulting feeling of dependence sometimes becomes intolerable and causes revolts. Further, gratitude for benefits psychologically produces minimum performance rather than greater effort.

3. Bargaining: "Let us agree that you will do as I say in certain respects, in return for which I will do what you want in certain other respects." Implied by each party is: "If you don't agree, I will prevent you from obtaining your objectives."[12]

All three methods are still widely used in school governance. Together, they describe much of the present state of professional staff relations in very many school systems. Ameliorated by common concern for children as it may be, the situation in professional employer-employee relations is widely felt to be growing worse rather than better. The three methods based on the assumed need for security do not achieve even satisfactory let alone optimum performance, because they are so far from satisfying any of the participants.

As McGregor points out, security has limitations as a motivator of performance: "A satisfied need is not a motivator of behavior. . . . After physiological needs [food, shelter, and physical welfare] are reasonably satisfied, needs at the next higher level begin to dominate man's behavior—to motivate him."[13] And when the next higher level of needs are satisfied, satisfaction of the next need level makes him dissatisfied, and so on. In rising order, these needs are: safety needs or fair treatment; social needs such as belonging and acceptance; the egoistic needs, for self-esteem and for status and recognition; and finally, the need for self-fulfillment, which is a continuing motivation.[14]

---

[12]Irving Knickerbocker, "Leadership: A Conception and Some Implications," *Journal of Social Issues*, Summer 1948; also in M. Chester Nolte (ed.), *An Introduction to School Administration: Selected Readings*, Macmillan, New York, 1966, pp. 130–132. © Copyright, M. Chester Nolte, 1966.

[13]Douglas McGregor, *The Human Side of Enterprise*, McGraw-Hill, New York, 1960; excerpted in Nolte, op. cit., p. 169.

[14]An order of values perhaps first described by Abraham Maslow; cf. his book entitled *Motivation and Personality*, Harper, New York, 1954.

Many managers whose governance is strictly hierarchic recognize the social and egoistic needs, but they fear that allowing those needs to be met—by allowing people to work in independent groups, for instance, or to share in decision making—would impair management objectives, even perhaps threaten management direction. Nevertheless it is possible to satisfy the needs for recognition and self-fulfillment, and thus utilize these motivations, through a fourth managerial method, that of mutually developed objectives.

This strategy entails a different view of human nature from that which assumes a dislike of work and a need for security. This view recognizes the higher order of needs and corresponding principles of human behavior:

1. Using physical and mental effort in work is as natural as it is in play.
2. External control and the threat of punishment are not the only means for bringing about effort toward organization objectives. Man will exercise self-direction and self-control in the service of objectives to which he is committed.
3. Commitment to objectives is related to the rewards associated with their achievement.
4. The average human being learns, under proper conditions, not only to accept but to seek responsibility.
5. The capacity to exercise a relatively high degree of imagination, ingenuity, and creativity in the solution of organizational objectives is widely, not narrowly, distributed in the population.
6. Under the conditions of modern industrial life, the intellectual potentialities of the average human being are only partially utilized.[15]

These principles are based on the expectation that human beings grow and develop in their work, rather than behave as so many cogs in a machine. Managers may conceive that a useful managerial strategy will be to use ingenuity in developing opportunities for people to find ways of realizing recognition and self-esteem, and fulfillment so far as possible, in activities which will advance managerial objectives. Sooner or later, however, a difference in objectives may emerge and the strategy may fail. If managers can recog-

[15]Nolte, op. cit., p. 176.

nize that the average human being is interested in developing the objectives of his or her activity and would be motivated in helping to solve the problems which touch those interests, it will make sense to involve people in the decisions by which they are affected. When the interests of those affected are involved in making operational decisions, those interests are also involved in supporting and promoting implementation.

Serious research on the role of human motivation in production began in business rather than in education. Soon after the turn of the century Mary Parker Follett wrote to business managers, "When you have made your employees feel that they are in some sense partners in the business, they do not improve the quality of their work, save waste in time and material, because of the Golden Rule, but because their interests are the same as yours."[16]

Follett saw coordination as the underlying strategy of effective organization:

> It seems to me that the first test of business administration, of industrial organization, should be whether you have a business with all its parts so co-ordinated, so moving together in their closely knit and adjusting activities, so linking, interlocking, interrelating, that they make a working *unit*—that is, not a congeries of separate pieces, but what I have called a functional whole or integrative unity.[17]

Considerably later, exceptionally high production in certain industries attracted attention during World War II and became the object of a number of postwar studies. McGregor, Likert,[18] Knickerbocker, and others cite instances of outstanding industrial production attributed to use of decision-sharing methods.

[16]Henry C. Metcalf and L. Urwick, *Dynamic Administration: The Collected Papers of Mary Parker Follett*, Harper & Brothers, New York, 1940, p. 82; quoted in Jacob W. Getzels, James M. Lipham, and Roald F. Campbell, *Educational Administration as a Social Process*, Harper & Row, New York, 1968, p. 32.

[17]Metcalf and Urwick, op. cit., p. 71; Getzels, Lipham, and Campbell, op. cit., p. 31.

[18]Rensis Likert, *New Patterns of Management*, McGraw-Hill, New York, 1961.

For those school administrators who may find it difficult to give up what they see as necessary control, Knickerbocker, writing of industry, observes that "this method has two positive consequences of tremendous importance.

> First, because it substitutes the possibility of increased need satisfaction, of many kinds, for the negative fear of reduced need satisfaction, it results in genuine motivation toward organizational objectives. The negative consequences of the first two methods [job control and paternalism] and of many examples of the third [collective bargaining]—restrictions of output, sabotage, hostility, resistance to change, etc.—vanish into thin air because their causes are removed. Second, this method taps the resources of the whole group. The successful leader of this kind soon discovers the tremendous potentialities for problem solving, for cost reduction, for improved methods, which remain largely latent in the group under other methods of leadership.
>
> Actually, because this method most closely approximates the "natural" relationship of functional leadership, it gives the leader, in the end, more rather than less control. His followers perceive him as a positive means to increased need satisfaction; instead of resenting his direction of their activities or accepting it passively, they seek it and encourage it. Reliance on personal power seldom if ever yields this result.[19]

In all the variety of personalities and situations which occur in organizations and systems across the country, no one management method is likely to be fully adopted. Rather, the whole spectrum of management theories which have been discussed is likely to appear in a myriad of combinations. A summary of management styles called the Managerial Grid was designed by Blake and Mouton, as shown in Figure 1.[20] Eighty-one management styles are scaled according to relative concern for people and relative concern for production. They range from the exertion of minimum effort for either

---

[19]Knickerbocker, op. cit.; also in Nolte, op. cit., p. 133.

[20]Robert R. Blake and Jane Srygley Mouton, *The Managerial Grid*, Gulf, Houston, 1964, p. 10.

FIGURE 1   Management Styles According to Relative
Concern for People and Relative Concern for
Production: The Managerial Grid

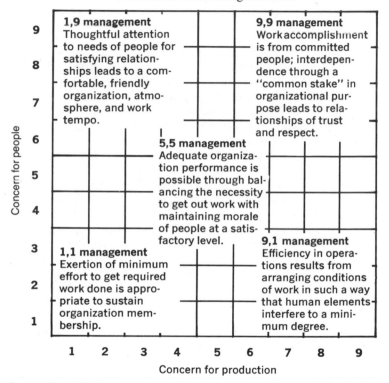

people or production to a situation of high productivity through common commitment and interdependence.

Management at the 1,1 level is described as "flabby," with relationship on a "give and take" basis. Many large organizations have managers at the 5,5 level; they use a "carrot and stick" approach and set achievable goals. Their people are likely to be tradition-directed and conditioned to bargaining.

Management at the 9,1 level will be recognized as assuming employee security as basic motivation, and at the 9,9 level as drawing upon the human motivation for self-fulfillment through shared objectives. Management at the 9,1 level in industry is frequently productive, but the strength of unions dedicated to security is attributed to reaction against such organizations and the desire to resist them. Among the descriptors of such organizations, open criticism is regarded as insubordination, the cardinal sin of all hierarchy. "Short-circuiting the boss" by going over his head (i.e., outside of channels) is strictly frowned upon. Disagreement is first cousin to insubordination, to be firmly suppressed.[21]

Management at the 9,9 level is characterized by effective integration of concern with people and concern with production, and becomes possible by involving the people and their ideas in determining the conditions and strategies of work. This is a partnership approach, and it is oriented toward discovering the best and most effective solutions, not those defined by tradition. Partnership managers enable goals to be established both by people who have the facts and by people who have stakes in the outcome. The assumption is that when the individuals who must carry out activities have real stakes in the outcome, direction and control are no longer necessary; people are self-directed and self-controlled in pursuit of the goals they have jointly adopted. Whereas people working under 9,1 management are typically in competition with fellow workers at the same level, because they are subject to the decisions of their superiors, under 9,9 management workers are equally involved in deciding objectives; thus conflict is obviated because competition is nonproductive.[22]

If we match these characteristics with those of open partnership, it is clear that 9,9 level of management is partnership governance because managers at that level use the partnership method of shared decision making; all those concerned or affected are involved in development of common objectives and in subsequent decisions as

[21]Ibid., pp. 38–46.
[22]Cf. ibid., p. 135.

needed. Because motivation is strong to fulfill one's own objectives and reap the benefits, joint efforts reach a high level of achievement.

LEADERSHIP IN A PARTNERSHIP STYLE

School administrators who are interested in moving in this more challenging direction will seek a leadership style that is effective in enabling their professional staffs to work most productively and the lay community to participate usefully and responsibly. The openness which is characteristic of collaborative styles is itself the means to defining roles, resolving conflicts, and organizing for functional structure, which are needs central to administration.

Opportunity to develop shared objectives is a first priority, pursued in part purposefully and in part as occasion offers. If the climate has been rather more hierarchic than open, teachers may be slow in offering ideas if they feel doing so runs a risk of touching someone's prerogative. The open administrator, however, can establish a practice of reaching out to people for ideas and encouraging people to develop their own roles in the collaborative process of identifying shared objectives.

In day-to-day operation effective leadership plays numerous roles, sometimes task specification, sometimes individual or group support. One successful principal of a well-established alternative high school says that the principal is basically not a decision maker, but the manager of the decision-making process. He implements the decisions in the sense that he sees that they are carried out, by whatever reminding and encouragement may be necessary. And while he carries a position of leadership by knowledge and experience, he says he is basically a stimulator, suggester, manager of resources, protector, and so on. Such skills take both interest and practice, but they are rather less tenuous and more substantial than prestige unaccompanied by solid personal relationships.

Likert found in studies of high-producing industries that they were six-to-one employee-centered rather than task-centered; that is, supervisors let people do their jobs the way they wished so long as they accomplished the agreed-upon objectives.[23] Sometimes, however, more flexible behavior is helpful, whether directive or supportive. Hersey and Blanchard have carried strategies of management behavior to meet varying situations to a degree of considerable sophistication.[24]

Openness which allows staff to find their own best working styles or their own work direction should not be confused with the prevalent isolation of teachers. An effective administrator may profitably arrange for better peer communication than obtains in most school systems. Likert describes studies of groups of research scientists which are pertinent to the question of self-direction. The studies concur in indicating that those scientists who made their own decisions independently from their chiefs and who did not see their chiefs daily were appreciably poorer in scientific performance than those scientists who had the same independence but did see their chiefs once a day. Active interest shown by the chiefs in ongoing work with a hands-off policy concerning direction—neither imposition of ideas nor isolation—marked the most fruitful leadership. Similarly, those scientists who were ''isolate'' and saw their colleagues less than two or three times a week were appreciably less productive than those who had more interaction. Freedom alone did not ensure performance, whereas interaction both provided stimulation and fostered creativity. Further research indicated that interaction of scientists with their chiefs' superiors was an additional useful stimulus.[25]

Encouragement of such ongoing interaction can lead to a collaborative climate in which individuals learn to trust each other. In this climate people will raise concerns which in a noncollaborative situation would be suppressed long enough to develop conflict. Questions can be talked out, with sharing of necessary information, before differences become jurisdictional and emotional.

Can this be applied to collective bargaining? The emotional

[23]Likert, op. cit., pp. 6–7.
[24]Paul Hersey and Kenneth H. Blanchard, *Management of Organizational Behavior*, Prentice-Hall, Englewood Cliffs, N.J., 1972.
[25]Likert, op. cit., pp. 23–25.

climate surrounding the whole question of professional negotiations is such that the suggestion of using collaborative methods to ease the situation is likely to draw skeptical reactions. Nevertheless, for hostility, for loss of peer relationships, and for elimination of the public interest, the situation is growing worse rather than better,[26] and some sort of remedy is badly needed.

One opening appears in a distinction between dealing with salaries and dealing with involvement in curriculum development and other professional interests. Where bargaining has been established for several years, it seems to have become accepted as a means for setting salaries. Where there is continuing dissatisfaction it generally stems from the wish of teachers to have a voice in the development of educational policies. Conflicts, and sometimes strikes, have arisen from school board (or administrative) decisions on school organization in which teachers felt they should have had a voice, and where there has been a signal lack of effort to identify common goals. Where both teachers and administration, as well as school boards, are unwilling to consider professional and humanistic questions at the bargaining table, with its attendant inflexibilities, the way may be opened to discussion of mutually developed objectives. If differences can be placed in a decision-sharing process, and open communications can be introduced, so that teachers may be directly involved where they are interested, differences are less likely to become crises and unproductive tensions may tend to disappear.

ADMINISTRATORS AND THE COMMUNITY

The process will not go far, however, before both administration and teachers realize that the community is also interested. Schools do not exist in a vacuum, and efforts to foster open communication within a school or school system will "curl at the edges" unless the community is closely involved. School people sometimes complain that the community is passive and uninterested, but if this were true there

[26]*Education U.S.A.*, Mar. 25, 1974, p. 165.

would be considerably less anxiety about "what the community will think." Indeed, observers sometimes feel that school governance is affected more often by fear of what the people will say than by actual disapproval. This is unfortunate, because community feeling about schools is generally supportive. Even the deep concerns about quality of education which citizens express are supportive at base. It is all too seldom recognized that people wish to know more about the schools, and many of them wish to be involved in improving schools. Many who are knowledgeable about education and about children want to offer ideas and to be able to engage in discussion about their ideas, preparatory to decision making, on such matters as curriculum, budget, school regulations, personnel qualifications, and other policy questions.

If there is any one real barrier to profitable community involvement in such discussions, that barrier is the deep-lying professional feeling of the lay-professional division, the feeling that schools belong to school people (especially the administration) and that the community role should be respectfully supportive, confined largely to funding a professionally determined budget. Even where administrators intellectually know better, community people are aware of subtle "put-downs" that keep them in their place. One high school principal listed such devices as emphasis on the value of credentials, reference to powerful allies in the community, appointment of a "commission to study education," and rejection of individual ideas with such a response as "too busy now" or "better things are happening elsewhere."

One commonly used device is frustrating to concerned citizens and sometimes a major pitfall for the administrator who uses it. That is the appointment of a selected representative committee or council. It is the rare administrator who appoints activists or known dissidents or other than "sound" and "reliable" individuals, and again the rare administrator who refrains from setting limits on the discussion. The result is that the deliberations and subsequent recommendations of such groups ignore a great deal of reality. The creation of such groups may serve to delay or avoid more pertinent activity, or cap temporarily a dissident movement, but they do not bring community people any closer to the schools or help existing tensions to disappear. Their support is no more real than any other facade.

On the other hand, if an open invitation were made to all who might be interested in a given question to come together to discuss it freely, the eventual recommendations of such a group would carry weight in both community and school. The administrator who wishes to achieve an open partnership can well begin by simply letting people join together to address problems, letting people help where perception of need is shared. Technical assistance to those involved is useful, so long as it centers on help in identifying objectives and relating activities to shared decisions. People are likely to respond to such invitations, just as they did for the "partnership schools" described in the second chapter. The reṡulting climate is warm and supportive, but more to the point, the common concern for the shared objectives develops a strong focus on student interests and on the quality of the educational program.

For instance, the directorate of the overseas dependents schools of the Department of Defense urged school principals to seek actively for "ways to form a true partnership with students, parents, teachers, and community members in the determination of school programs and priorities." The director emphasized: "The community and the parents have the right to review the process of the educational program. . . . How this review takes place should be determined locally."

A detailed list of possibilities followed, which included the role of "silent communicators" in making people feel welcome in the school, and the reminder that "community involvement should be regarded as a process, not a set of accommodations, and that due process must be observed in making any changes to the school program."[27] The school-community partnership program in the dependents schools was begun in the spring of 1973. It may or may not be

[27]USDESEA, *Community Involvement in USDESEA*, Department of the Army, Directorate, United States Dependents Schools, European Area, APO 09164, Pamphlet No. 360-6, Sept. 1, 1975.

related that when Congress proposed to cut the schools' appropriation in the fall of 1975, parents wrote more than ten thousand letters within thirty days in protest.[28]

Such a process will also serve those administrators who are concerned about pressures for "accountability" in the quantitative sense. If school and community people have developed shared objectives which are appropriately broad, school achievement in fulfilling such objectives cannot be measured simply in quantitative ways. Rather, in the process of considering current school activity as a part of developing objectives, school personnel will be accounting for what they do to those most closely concerned, and thereby building collaboration and support where it counts the most.

Openness in others cannot be mandated, no more than can collaboration, but it can be modeled, invited, and encouraged simply by accepting a host of everyday opportunities. Examples of third-party interventions which have fostered openness in schools are plentiful. For instance, the first changes in the highly traditional Boston schools came largely from the community-initiated introduction of school volunteers. With their eager, imaginative helpfulness and careful training for acceptable intervention, they made appreciable changes not only in that rather austere climate but in developing libraries and other new facilities which influenced the curriculum. Most of all, perhaps, their one-to-one working with children opened new horizons for many students. They were forerunners of teachers' aides who freed many frustrated and able teachers for long-desired enterprises.

The innovative federal program called Teacher Corps has initiated lasting transformations in many schools through its unorthodox in-service preparation methods. These methods include interaction with the community—taking teachers into the community and bringing community people into the school—which greatly increases student and teacher understanding of each other. In one New

---

[28]*PTSA News and Views*, European Congress of American Parents, Teachers, and Students, December-January 1976.

England city a Teacher Corps team so impressed the school administration with its ability to improve teacher-student relationships that existing in-service education was redesigned in the Teacher Corps pattern. In another city, a team involved community people in changing an elementary school curriculum from a traditional program to a program with traditional and open alternatives.

In a suburban school a new administrative assistant brought teachers together for unaccustomed but successful planning—a simple thing, it seems, but an intervention that began a much-needed transformation in faculty communication. A PTA study group of parents and teachers met every other week during the school year to discuss chapters of Haim Ginott's book entitled *Between Parent and Child*.[29] Among other outcomes, the primary teachers in the group applied for and received permission to introduce vertical or family groupings in their classrooms. The venture was successful and later extended to upper grades. When the New England Program in Teacher Education held a series of teacher workshops in educational innovation, teachers brought their principals, and aides brought teachers, saying, "This is what I was trying to tell you about."

Undoubtedly thousands of instances could be collected of third-party contributions, both lay and professional, which have led to better communications and more responsive programs. Practically all of them would have in common the natural colleagueship of people concerned about children and their education, willingness to collaborate, and at least the temporary freedom to do so. The school administrator who looks for greater "cooperation" from teachers, students, and community can use the myriad of opportunities for "people involvement" that are always presenting themselves.

Perhaps more administrators would utilize these opportunities if they felt that fostering involvement led to change without unexpected and possibly unpleasant complications. Underlying such administrative caution is experience with community opposition to school programs, and perhaps with ill-advised community ventures. These ex-

---

[29]Haim Ginott, *Between Parent and Child*, Macmillan, New York, 1965.

periences tend to develop resistance to an easy acceptance of student-teacher-community involvement. The key to these difficulties can generally be traced to an incorrect assumption of common objectives. The first priority in any instance, therefore, is to bring together those who are concerned to identify common objectives for the contemplated enterprise. It is important that the identification be agreed to and clearly understood by all, even though the objectives may change somewhat as the enterprise proceeds.

It is further important that the objectives as identified become a continuing reference in evaluation of progress, and that the evaluation include a check on whether all those who may be affected by the project as it grows have been invited to participate. These steps will prevent the neglect of "tag ends" in a project which may have unpleasant side effects. If all those arc involved in a project who should be involved, continuing evaluation leads to a substantial part of the community accounting for its own activity and therefore in the best sense sharing responsibility for the partnership program.

SUMMARY

The argument of this chapter is that administrators can bring about higher performance in their schools when they support individual interests for self-fulfillment than by the coercive or manipulative measures characteristic of hierarchic management. Schools are more effective with their students when administrators enable faculty, staff, students, and interested citizens to involve themselves in educational matters in behalf of their own concerns for better education. The required administrative leadership lies in enabling all of these to join in identifying common objectives within the existing framework of school structure, goals, and role assignments, accepting growth and change in structure and goals through developmental activity among all of those concerned.

Such leadership assists individuals in self-fulfillment and provides for interaction among peers and between various role groups, without imposing programs; a continuing attention to common objectives will maintain quality of educational program and focus on student interests. In this way administrators find that their own goals and the goals of individuals involved are very similar if not pretty much one and the same.

Involved in this leadership also is the ability to avoid divisiveness between groups by bringing them together, to allay board-teacher or administration-teacher rivalries, and to support school board communications with all groups. In the current professional climate this often means that administrators need to set an example of regard for lay judgment and lay contribution, and for the value of community initiative.

While any of the component groups involved in a school system can initiate efforts to bring about a collaborative climate, some are in better positions to achieve substantial success than others. School administrators are in the best position of all, not because of a power situation but because they are the key to the communications system of their schools or school district. In this position their influence reaches beyond that of any other group.

CHAPTER FIVE

What the Partnership Idea Can Mean to Teachers

IN TODAY'S SCHOOLS teachers as well as many administrators are seeking relationships more pertinent to professional status. Their frustrations about relationships are different from those of administrators, but perhaps even more bewildering. McPherson aptly summarized one teacher's conception of her "place":

> The core of the teacher's self-image was its moral obligation. To teach was to serve; it was not just to earn a living. . . . Her picture of herself as performing a moral duty did not blind her to evidence that she had little prestige and power in school and community. Recognizing this low esteem, she had to struggle for dignity and self-respect. . . . The four major strands of the Adams teacher's self-image were as disciplinarian, as director of learning, as industrious worker, and as one deserving just and equitable treatment.[1] . . . [T]he teacher's conviction [was] that the school environment was hostile, that she was surrounded by enemies, and that she needed protection.[2]

The name of the town is fictional, but the teacher exists, probably in the hundreds of thousands, if one may trust a myriad of formal and informal interviews by or known to this writer over a number of

---

[1]Gertrude H. McPherson, *Small Town Teacher*, Harvard, Cambridge, Mass., *1972, p. 29. Copyright* © 1972 by president and fellows of Harvard College.
[2]Ibid., p. 53.

years. There are at least as many "strands" in the teacher's relationships to the school society about him or her as correspond loosely to the strands in his or her self-image: relationships to the students, to their parents, to colleagues, and to superiors, that is, the administration and the school board.

The first of these strands, relationship with students, is obviously the teacher's reason for being, and the core of the whole. Of the other three strands, it is especially by the fourth and most peripheral relationship—that with school boards and administrators—that teachers are best known to the general public, and because of increasing confrontation the whole picture is in risk of distortion.

Teachers first addressed this relationship with purpose when the century-old National Education Association (NEA) took organizational action for teachers' rights. As West put it at the outset of the decade which saw the rise of professional negotiations:

> The signs of the middle 1960's are clear: The elementary and secondary public school teachers of the United States are in a state of ferment bordering on rebellion. Almost every day in some way in some school district the symptoms of this condition are starkly revealed. Some of the symptoms are: an official declaration by a teachers' association that educational standards in a school system are so bad that no self-respecting teacher should continue to make his services available, an illegal strike, a street demonstration, a refusal to perform extracurricular activities, and similar self-help techniques that are characteristic of social revolutions. The phenomenon is all the more startling since it fits neither the tradition nor the image of the American public school teacher.[3]

It was not merely the low salaries, large classes, lack of services, and inadequate materials, equipment, and supplies that caused resentment, West continued, but the "regimentation" of public school teachers. Along with academic improvement in teacher preparation had come a sense of professionalism which changed their view of themselves.

[3]Alan M. West, What's Bugging Teachers," *Saturday Review*, Oct. 16, 1965, p. 88.

They insist that professionalism gives them rights as well as responsibilities—the right to exercise professional judgment, the right to a voice in the selection of teaching materials, to help plan the curriculum, to have the rights of full partners in making those decisions that affect the conditions under which teachers teach and children learn. . . .

They rebel at those regimental systems that exist too often in our large cities where the week's lesson plan must meet a prescribed standard enforced by a subject matter supervisor who rates performance on the basis of adherence to plan rather than how much pupils learn. They demand the right to influence the school board and superintendent on policy matters.

Finally, they understand that, in the large depersonalized school systems of today created by urbanization and consolidation, the professional rights they claim can only be exercised effectively through collective action.[4]

Even though bargaining is in a way itself a recognition of hierarchic governance, insistence upon bargaining has played a major role in redressing the hierarchic balance. Professional negotiations have brought about a considerable increase in the teachers' share in policy making. On the other hand, success for teachers has often led to increased militancy among school boards and to situations which have gone beyond the desired decision sharing to the crystallizing of adversary positions. In a Newtonian sort of action-reaction process, one intransigent and exclusionary action surpasses another, so that hostilities tend to rise and differences between staff and school board are more difficult to resolve after agreements have been reached. The growth of an industrial, hierarchic process among a professional group who are also in public service, while historically justified, has become an anomaly—and because of the sharp differences on the collision point of strikes, a sore anomaly. The questions about strikes cannot be resolved, in this writer's view, by looking to patterns of other employment relationships, whether public or private. Each has its own set of conditions under which relationships must be resolved.

[4]Ibid.

Teachers find themselves in a difficult situation: when school boards and administrators draw together in adversary positions, teachers feel the need of their own organizations. On the other hand, the greater teacher dependence upon their organization becomes, and the greater the adversary pressures, the more rigid and protective an organizational structure is likely to become, and the more inflexible to change. As rigidity increases, if the pattern follows that of the industrial craft unions, access to the profession may also become restricted, with resulting ill effect for all who are concerned with and involved in education. Altogether, it is a situation which can hardly be cured without a general recognition of equality between teaching staff, administration, and elected boards, each in their respective roles sharing in the development of compatible educational policy.

TEACHER ISOLATION

As to relationships among teachers, the next inner strand in the teacher's social system, the organizations have been partially effective in bringing teachers together in a feeling of colleagueship. Large numbers who do not participate in organizational activities, and are not altogether happy with a militant stance, do willingly pay substantial dues to their organizations as a needed safeguard to their welfare. Also, the organizations are in many cases broadening their activities and providing educational services to their members, which helps to reduce teacher isolation.

Nevertheless, isolation is still the hallmark of relationships among teachers, based on the well-established code that a teacher is not to be interfered with in his or her own classroom. Once the door is closed, within those four walls the teacher is beyond reach. Teachers do not visit one another's classrooms, or criticize one another; neither do they countenance criticism of other teachers, for that could lead to criticism of themselves.

The ideal role-expectation that any Adams teacher held of a colleague was that she show loyalty. A teacher who betrayed another to class or parent was resented.[5] . . . The new teachers, with their unfamiliar and varied backgrounds, appeared to adhere to strange methods of teaching and even to set themselves somewhat different goals. In so doing they challenged the traditional methods and upset the ritualistic security on which much of the Old Guard philosophy rested. . . . If she did not interfere or help, the new teacher would finally accept defeat: "She'll learn." Until the new teacher could talk her language, could look at teaching in her terms, she could not be trusted or confided in. But on the other hand, suppose the new teacher went too far in upsetting the old order, as she might without enough supervision? Maybe something had to be done by the Old Guard teacher to socialize her. From these contradictory pressures to interfere and to keep hands off emerged a pattern of indirect training through innuendo and hint, accompanied by strong hostility when this approach failed to change the new teacher's behavior.[6]

Under this prevailing protocol, individual teachers have developed outstanding programs, highly innovative and educative in nature; they may have been recognized by both public press and educational journals; but their work has seldom been adapted by others in their own schools. Teachers or administrators from other communities may inquire, but commonly not the teachers next door. The work Robert Gillette was doing in Andrew Warde High School in Fairfield, Connecticut, with "turned-off" students was recognized by his colleagues and by his students' parents, but shared by only one other teacher until he received the Gresham Chair award of $100,000.[7] That other teacher, incidentally, initiated the grant application. Only subsequently did other teachers in his own community come with their dreams for consultation and help, as well as hundreds from other school districts and other states. Gillette was able to

[5]McPherson, op. cit., p. 53.

[6]Ibid., p. 66.

[7]Robert Gillette was holder of the Gresham Chair, which carried a three-year grant of $100,000 awarded to the New England teacher who produced a plan "offering the richest learning resources to students in cooperation with school and community" by the New England Program in Teacher Education, from 1972–1975.

bring about change by being placed in a leadership role and because he exercised leadership in a collaborative manner with other teachers.

As we have seen, administrators are in a strong position to bring about collaboration among teachers. Yet it remains a curious paradox that people who claim professional status, and the sense of inquiry and discriminating judgment which professional status implies, are content to wait upon designated leadership or outside agents to bring them together in collaboration.

WHOSE CHILD?

Closest to the primary teacher-student relationship is that between teachers and parents. It is commonly called a natural partnership, attested by well over three-quarters of a century of parent-teacher associations in practically all schools. Actually, there are few relationships more complicated with emotions. The fact that parents and teachers are both concerned with socialization, education, and the best interests of the child does not eliminate the fundamental difference in their relationships or the difference in their expectations.

> Although the teacher wanted support and respect, her own expectations for the parents made it impossible for her to give the parents what would produce this support and respect. The core of the teacher's expectation was that a parent respond as the teacher did, to be universalistic, which meant to be objective, rational, and realistic about the child. The teacher believed that few parents lived up to this basic demand.[8]

Parents' requests for help are often taken as they were in the case of the Adams teacher, as "backhanded criticism, which made her defensive and hostile, or as true humility, which encouraged her to humiliate the parent even more. The teacher was usually put on the defensive in a parent-initiated contact, and the parent was put on the defensive in a teacher-initiated contact."[9] Despite an increasing

[8]McPherson, op. cit., p. 134.
[9]Ibid., p. 130.

number of handbooks and attention in teacher education courses, the positive elements in most parent-teacher conferences are still outweighed by the negative.

The frequency with which attendance at PTA meetings has become an item in professional negotiations—distressing to lay leaders who regard PTA as a wholly voluntary organization—suggests that teacher-parent relationships are sometimes regarded as more problematical than helpful. Late in 1968 *The PTA Magazine*, through a survey of its readers, collected grievances of parents with teachers and of teachers with parents and published representative samples. Parents were concerned about unsafe playgrounds, unsupervised playgrounds, inadequate cafeterias, inadequate curriculum, poor equipment, unwillingness of principals to hear ideas, icy reception in parent-teacher conferences, being "told" instead of consulted. Teachers complained of parental disbelief in a child's limitations, parents' requests to give their children extra help, parent pressure for better grades, parent excuses for poor work, parent tantrums, parental belief of the child's story when a difference arises, parental apathy in improving schools.

The long list of grievances bespeaks not only general lack of collaboration between the prime movers in a child's life, but poor communication. It suggests that parents and teachers do not know each other as people. When the teachers' chief contact with the community is with the parents, and the parents who know the school mainly through their child's teacher are the core of school support in the community, the implications are not reassuring.

This pervasive distrust between parents and teachers helps to account for the uneasiness which talk of accounting for educational achievement has created among teachers and other educators. When teachers widely distrust parents' views of their own children's needs, they would also tend to distrust public understanding of what is measurable achievement and what is not. If the public does indeed have so little understanding of schools as educators appear to believe, it can only be attributed to the walls which have been raised between schools and their communities.

TEACHING AND LEARNING

We come to the fourth and central strand of the teacher's relationships, that with the student as "disciplinarian and director of learning." Here, if anywhere in this collaborative business of education, we should find the mutuality of concern for learning. To the contrary, however, we find that for the most part the hierarchic pattern of superior-inferior relationships still obtains.

> The goal sought by the teacher, that the pupils learn, that they achieve a definite academic level during the course of the school year, was basic, but its accomplishment was only justified in the teacher's eyes if it was achieved through the legitimated means of docility and effort.[10]

Only in very recent years has this attitude toward students become openly recognized as a factor in learning. The publication of *Pygmalion in the Classroom*[11] in 1968 sparked heated debate and counterclaims. A succession of documented experiences have supported the thesis that teacher expectations do affect student learning. The reverse Pygmalion effect demands the greater concern, of course: that is, that students are deterred from learning by a teacher's low estimate of their abilities.[12] Some British research indicates that teachers' attitudes influence not only students' academic performance but their friendships and perhaps their futures as well.

> Nash studied 152 pupils who were transferred from different elementary schools to a single larger school on the outskirts of Edinburgh. Within a short time, nearly all had joined cliques, based not only on social class or intelligence, but on how their teachers had acted toward them. . . .
> The children are now in what the British call "unstreamed" classes. Later they will be divided into three "banded streams" on the basis of scholastic ability. . . . "It is as near a

[10]Ibid., p. 84.

[11]Robert Rosenthal and Lenore Jacobson, *Pygmalion in the Classroom: Teacher Expectation and Pupils' Intellectual Development*, Holt, New York, 1968.

[12]Cf. Jere E. Brophy and Thomas L. Good, "Teacher Expectations: Beyond the Pygmalion Controversy," *Phi Delta Kappan*, December 1972, pp. 276–278.

sociological certainty as anything can be,'' says Nash, ''that most of the boys in clique 1 are headed for band 1, those in clique 2 for band 2, and those in clique 3 for band 3. It is the children in clique 3 who will become increasingly difficult as they become older and who will need the most teaching.''[13]

The overwhelming feeling among students and parents is that most teachers do not really know their students other than by behavior, with notable exceptions, and there is little evidence in the literature of teacher education to counter this view. The common assumption is that knowing every student personally would be more than time and energy would allow. Until fairly recently most parents and students accepted this situation, whether they liked it or not.

As understanding the learning process becomes more important, however, the question becomes more insistent: if teachers do not know their students, or know them very little, is it not hard to tell when they are learning and when they are encountering problems? Classroom tests can tell when they *have* encountered problems, but not necessarily where the difficulty lies. Children are so adaptable that they are generally able to take a teacher's direction and turn it to use by their own learning methods; yet it is obvious that as a *teaching* method direction falls short.

A teacher's friendly and approving behavior to a child will help the child think well of himself, but the teacher's behavior to a child is freighted with more than effect on his self-image. When a teacher knows a child well enough to think of him or her as another human being, the teacher's attitude, and style of teaching as well, undergoes a subtle change. The child is no longer a sort of living puppet to be placed according to plan, kept under control but moving, but a person with opinions and ideas to which the teacher feels response, and therefore a person to whom a certain respect must be paid. The child is inevitably enlivened and responsive. Treating a person with respect is very close to treating him or her with equality. It was perhaps with something of this sort in mind that the director of the U.S. Depen-

[13]Peter Watson, European Correspondent, report on research of Roy Nash, North Wales Univesity College, in *Behavior Today*, Dec. 17, 1973.

dents Schools, European Area, serving some 115,000 students, advised the school principals of the area as follows:

> New ways of dealing with students may be much more educative than any change we might make in curriculum, and sometimes changes in administrative structure and changes in curriculum may not make much difference if we don't find the right way to deal with students. I ask you, is it possible for us to establish a relationship with students where we consider them as equals? I'm not really sure that in the end establishment of students as equals with teachers and administrators might not be a more educative thing for the students than anything else we might do. I think unfortunately what we have done too often is consider the rights of the institution, the school, if you will, as a passer-on of the culture rather than as a place where we may practice the techniques of releasing the creative energies of children. It's quite possible that the great emphasis we place on conformity and the rules we make are not in keeping with our objectives of developing the individual.[14]

Thus it may not be so much knowing the student well as it is the quality of the relationship which makes the difference in student learning. Being treated as equal causes any person to rise in self-esteem, and causes most of us to respond with greater responsibility. Treating students as equals would amount to taking them into partnership in the educative process, and thus actually sharing responsibility for learning. Teaching would become a less one-sided affair. Some teachers would feel the loss of a sense of control, analogous to that which the school administrator might feel in sharing responsibility with teachers. Some teachers might also distrust their own abilities to manage a classroom without accustomed controls. They will find, however, that by entering into partnership teachers have not abrogated the emphasis on mutual respect; they will have increased that emphasis. It does mean a difference in dealing with children: it means honest dealing, which may entail

[14]Joseph A. Mason, Director, U.S. Dependents Schools, European Area, address to USDESEA Administrators' Conference, Berchtesgaden, Germany, October 1971.

difficulties for some adults. It means abandoning manipulation through loaded questions, a habit many adults have acquired in a defensive society, in favor of encouraging objective thinking on the part of the students.

One of the "partnership schools" described in Chapter Two, Westminster West, particularly impressed its observers by the responsibility which the students assumed for their own learning, a responsibility seen to derive from their treatment as individuals. Very young students often initiated learning and teaching procedures, materials, and fairly complex mechanisms.

When teachers understand that children, like any normal people, work with a sense of purpose, their expectation of purpose in children's learning activities becomes a motivating influence. When teachers evaluate their students' work in terms of fulfillment of the students' own purposes, teachers are contributing to growth of responsibility. Moreover, they are to some degree accounting to students for their own part in the teaching-learning process.[15]

Such a different view of teaching opens the door to partnership with all the components of a school society. When the student is recognized as a partner in rather than the object of the educational enterprise, the relationship between parent and teacher changes. The necessary concern for both becomes that of relating to the student's own purposes, so that the supposed conflict between their two points of view tends to disappear.

Perrone and Strandberg describe experiences which may encourage the skeptical teacher in this course:

> Three years of rather intensive discussion with several thousand parents in communities throughout North Dakota and other parts of the United States has made us skeptical of the knowledge most school officials possess of parental interest in education. Some of our initial meetings with parents were awkward—it was the first time many of them had talked about

[15]Cf. Vito Perrone and Warren Strandberg, "A Perspective on Accountability," *Teachers College Record*, February 1972.

educational issues. But interaction with these people has provided us with more insights into education than we ever gained in our professional training. They clearly recognize that children are different, that they learn in different ways and have different interests, and they believe that schools should affirm this basic understanding in practice. They are sensitive to the effects on children of rejection and failure. Their awareness that a separation existed between the school and the home—that what children were about in school did not carry over into the home, and that children's interests at home were not beginning points for study at school—was enlightening. For them, it was simply "common sense" that such activities should intersect, and that such an intersection would cause their children to become more interested in school.[16]

The "intersection" of student activities is an easy opening to a conjunction between parents and teachers. It can be casual and informal, sharing information, sharing activities if desired. It has long seemed to the writer that the most useful method of accounting for school performance is one of continuing collaboration, accounting in day-to-day operations for what happens in school in any area that arouses interest, whatever the performance may have been.[17]

It often happens that when parents and teachers begin to collaborate as individuals, they find that their shared interest in the students leads into dealing with other shared concerns, such as alcohol or drug abuse, juvenile offenders, or child neglect, which allow both parents and teachers to set aside their ordinary roles and work together as individuals with different expertise. In such activity teachers and parents gain a respect for one another's strengths that carries over into a substantive colleagueship. It is a relationship which immeasurably improves the learning climate for students. It also creates far-reaching change in classrooms.

The students and teachers who operate in the four-walled classroom, that is, in isolation, develop the conviction that other groups

[16]Ibid., p. 348.
[17]Charlotte Ryan, *The State Dollar and the Schools*, Massachusetts Advisory Council on Education, Boston, 1970, pp. 21–22.

are unimportant, no matter what the subject matter of the curriculum says. Students learn to be individualistic, competitive, and also prejudiced—because they have no opportunity to learn by experience how groups are interrelated and dependent on one another. So they grow up in isolation, and when they leave school they take their walls along with them.

On the other hand, building a school-community interaction in which teachers are active participants, as individuals, along with students and other citizens, helps students to understand how they relate to other parts of the society to which they belong. In developing cooperative skills, which are the basis of cooperative living, students grow up with less suspicion, less competitiveness, less prejudice, and they are more inclined to take responsibility wherever they are because they have more trust in others as well as in themselves. This is particularly important where some segments of the community tend to insist on isolation, as some ethnic groups are prone to do. Cultural heritages are not thereby disparaged; more probably they are recognized and enhanced. Thus doubly enriched, the influence of such education holds particular significance in a period when society is under conflicting strains, and reacts increasingly toward less individual responsibility and more centrist public policies.

BUILDING THE POSITIVE CLIMATE

A group of principals and teachers attending a "Teachers' Woodstock"[18] in Fairfield, Connecticut, expressed frustration in their attempts at change in their own schools. It developed in discussion that most of those present had worked in some sort of task force to bring about change, but the groups had in each case been limited to those with common interests and were lacking in both dissidents and decision makers.

It is usual for those who wish to bring about change to bring

[18]Workshop under leadership of Robert Gillette, June 22–24, 1973.

together those who are like-minded to develop their strategies. The underlying thought seems to be, "There is time enough to test our proposal with others when we have worked it out for ourselves, when we have perfected it." In thus limiting themselves, however, groups commonly overlook significant factors which dissidents could have pointed out. When it is later recognized that other factors must be dealt with, it is more difficult to weave the necessary solutions into the fabric of a proposal which is nearly completed. It may then be impossible to gain necessary support of others who were not there. The first rule in collaboration for change is to involve all who may be concerned or affected, as a matter of course.

The resulting development of a collaborative climate allows opportunities to be used as they arise. One delightful incident, which occurred in Princeton, N.J., is a case in point:

The idea for Riverside's "little switch" just seemed to rise like a cloud out of an ordinary Monday faculty meeting. An exhausted teacher had groaned something like "You can't appreciate the schedule I have. You ought to be in my shoes, put in a day like I just put in" and a bemused staff [Lou Cicchini] responded with "That's not a bad idea." An experiment grew out of this exchange.

"I collected all the names in a hat," says Norma Gumbiner. "Everybody who wanted to took part." . . . Almost the whole staff eventually joined in. . . . After the first collection of names, Norma went around again and everybody drew a new identity. .

Everybody agrees that there was a gay holiday spirit in the building that day. Kids were aware that there was lots of laughter and good feeling. Teachers commented that the kids rose to the occasion, took events in stride, and were very helpful in explaining the schedules they were accustomed to follow, picking up on their own work and making themselves agreeable and cooperative.

Afterward the sentiment among staff members was that the experiment was a great success and should be tried again for a longer period of time. . . . "I had a ball," says Christa Rounds. "It was the greatest way to become principal in a hurry. It gave me an insight into how much has to be done within a limited time. . . ." "There's a great value in kids seeing adults in other roles than the ones they're accustomed to," says Jetta Hall. . . . Barbara Bass . . . marked a very real difference in the kinds of teaching methods that would be effective with children of different ages. . . . Marilyn Shteir found, "For one thing, they're taller. That seems a funny and obvious thing to say, but when they come up to you, you see their eyes. That immediately gives you a different perspective." . . . "It made people a little more empathetic about each other's jobs, said Elaine Marshall. . . . Edith Francis says, "It left us all with good friendly feelings."[19]

This incident involved practically the whole school. It could not have happened without the concurrence of the principal— more, without the understanding that the principal would concur. It cannot be stressed too often that the willingness or unwillingness of those concerned to involve themselves in a program and, equally, to involve others concerned, determines the quality of the climate and dynamics of any social system. For teachers the quality of the school's climate strongly affects their ability to operate.

Two contrasting incidents illustrate this point quickly. In a New England city school system a directive came from the central office that the four social studies teachers in a junior high school were to undertake team teaching. According to one of the four teachers involved, one of the group was interested, one was opposed, and the other two were "willing." No steps were taken for orientation, however, or for any sort of discussion, and literally nothing happened. Two years later the directive was withdrawn, again without explanation. In this instance the teachers involved felt no freedom or incentive for taking initiative, even to call each other together for an exploratory discussion.

Telfer relates a similar incident in which a science guide had been developed in the "front office" and issued with a directive for its use; the guide was ignored. Some months later a newly appointed

[19] *Wednesday*, vol. 7, no. 5, Princeton Public Schools, Princeton, N.J., Feb. 6, 1974.

director of instruction assessed the situation and in a group meeting simply asked the teachers for suggestions about science instruction in general. Within minutes a committee of volunteers was formed to write another guide.[20]

A Kettering Foundation research project focused on this precise point: what are motivating influences toward improving the status quo? Of eight schools studied, teachers in only one school were found "who cared enough about the goals and values of the school and felt enough sense of control and power to modify and improve them on a continuous basis." In this school the teachers enjoyed two supportive influences in particular: the school and its community were found to hold similar values, and the principal encouraged their desire for improvement. The observers concluded:

> When a principal is consciously aware of his teachers' professional qualifications to instruct children, there is a much greater opportunity for the school as a unit to attain its desired objectives. If, on the other hand, the principal is more concerned with making a good impression on the district superintendent, maintaining his role as the authority figure, and pushing his faculty for productive output, there is less opportunity for faculty involvement and, therefore, the organizational renewal process will suffer.[21]

Influences upon the teacher from beyond the school building, from superintendent and school board, differ only in being removed from the daily scene. As influences on quality of teaching they are beneficent or counterproductive in the same manner as the building principal may be: whether they are "maintaining [a] role as authority figure, and pushing [the] faculty for productive output," or encouraging their "teachers' professional qualifications to instruct children." If the partnership is to be valid, moreover, it must deal with the question of professional negotiations. It seems to this writer

[20]Richard G. Telfer, "Staff Involvement: Key to Curriculum Improvement," *The Clearing House*, May 1969, p. 539 ff.

[21]Richard C. Williams, Charles C. Wall, W. Michael Martin, and Arthur Berchin, *Effecting Organizational Renewal in Schools: A Social Systems Perspective*, McGraw-Hill, New York, 1974, pp. 40–41, 70.

that the legal responsibilities of school boards and the interests of teacher organizations in sharing decisions about assignments, curricula, and working conditions are not really at odds. One must recognize that both superintendent and school board are conscious of the community looking over their shoulders, as it were; the only recourse, and the appropriate action, is to involve the community as well in the partnership.

Among several instances in which just this action of involving the community has occurred is one which stemmed from the initiative of a state education association president, Louise Jones of Idaho. Mrs. Jones wrote a general letter to the superintendents of the state suggesting an inquiry for an alternative to the industrial model for professional negotiations. Subsequent correspondence with the superintendent of the Independent School District of Boise City led to a cooperative program over some 2½ years which involved teachers, administrators, students, and other citizens. The starting point from each perspective was, "What do I want from the Boise schools?" Groups at each school met at two-week intervals. Starting with butcher paper to list every possible problem, they continued in the process to develop priorities and goals. Decisions were made by school staff, students, and community people, with the principal assuming the role of facilitator rather than director. A district council of representatives from each of the schools brought their ideas together and kept all groups informed. The final outcome was a model of decentralized administration and decision making. The superintendent wrote with some enthusiasm:

> Budget, evaluation—certainly with participation of students, student council, the PTA, or whatever other group—are important functions. When you visualize what may take place in the second year with the whole recycling, with the involvement of the community, the principal, and the staff having a "feel" for the total process, you can see the concept begin to function. At this point, the goals of the institution and the objectives of the individual become one, and this is the essence of the model. . . .

We have an example at one school where, unless the principal sits down with at least ninety parents at that school (that is practically the total parent count for the particular grade level) monthly, and with his faculty to explain what is going on in the school, he knows the program will fail.

We don't think that the concept is going to negate the need for negotiations; we simply think that it is going to place the emphasis on negotiation in an entirely different light.[22]

EVALUATION AND TRUST

Two fast-growing developments would seem to make imperative such broad efforts to enable the various members of the school community to learn trust of one another to the point of active colleagueship. These developments are outside and beyond the question of teacher strikes. One is the movement catch-phrased as "accountability": the cost-based conviction spreading across the country that schools should account for what they do in terms of student achievement.

The other movement stems largely from a long-standing organizational concern that teachers become responsible for competence within their own ranks, but it has become involved in the public pressure toward accounting for educational achievement. This is the movement for evaluation of teachers in their classroom performance for certification, for employment, and for salary increases. It comes to action on legislative floors just at the time when costs are a greater public concern than quality of education, when education holds relatively low political status and its problems are less likely to attract public sympathy, and when institutional hostilities between teachers and school boards have not yet abated.

Evaluations of teaching competence are of course made all the time by school administrators, for various purposes. After a great deal of political activity, in which not only the teachers but other

[22]Stephenson S. Youngerman, Jr., *The Decentralized Administrative Concept*, A Report to the Board of Trustees, Boise City Independent School District, Boise, Idaho, Jan. 3, 1972.

professional organizations have been involved, new laws enacted in several states require that evaluation for certification be substantially by peers. The questions of what competencies shall be evaluated have nowhere yet been resolved. As Pitman points out:

> A paradox of sorts is generated. Competency-based certification necessitates specific evaluation of competencies selected, which is certainly better, in terms of the value collected, than vague and global measures. Less vague measures should be less subject to subjective judgments and arbitrary decisions. However, as one develops more specific competencies and consequently focuses evaluations, the more important the selection of competencies becomes. . . . In effect, the argument shifts from the actual measurement techniques employed to more general value questions which may be extremely subjective. If the foregoing is valid, a major implication is that effective use of broadly based consortia is essential for developing a consensus on values so that evaluation procedures can be developed from a common value base.[23]

Pitman's argument poses the necessity of collaboration as a base for any evaluation procedure, if only because there must be agreement on values for the outcome of evaluation to be acceptable. For the individuals being evaluated, and for teachers generally, there must be trust in both colleagues and process if the new procedure is to be tolerable. One can only guess at the discomfiture that would be created in schools by a certification process that was not trusted. It is all the more important, therefore, to recognize that the expectation of fair and perceptive treatment, as the Adams teacher put it, can be met only through the kind of trust that is created by involvement in collaboration—collaboration which is not limited to certification questions.

The law may mandate evaluation by peers, and some legal body may be empowered to detail procedures, but collaborative processes

[23]John C. Pitman, *Summary of Actions Taken by Selected States Involved in Developing Competency-based Certification Systems*, New England Program in Teacher Education, Durham, N.H., August 1973.

are not susceptible to mandate. The change from separatist to collaborative habits occurs in individuals much as learning occurs; it is an interactive process. It is facilitated by small groups in which individuals learn habits of equal partnership. It can be encouraged, particularly if teachers are granted the incentives of determining their own goals—both professional and personal. It is assisted both by official approval and by skill counseling as desired. But the learning experience is individual; what one individual or group has learned may not be transferred to another.

Thus, if consensus on values as a part of the certification procedure is allowed to depend on some formal statement taken at state level, much as states have promulgated goals for education to local school districts, the procedure will almost certainly fail. It is the process by which individuals reach consensus, the sharing of views and perspectives, and the growth of ideas toward consensus, which develops trust in the evaluation based on the values agreed upon. Therefore it is indispensable to the evaluation procedure that the evaluators and the teacher evaluated share the process of reaching consensus.

To those who expect that teams will be appointed to evaluate teacher candidates for certification in the manner that schools are now commonly evaluated for accreditation, such a procedure could well seem logistically impossible. The fundamental difference is that certification should be, not a gateway to be held or an obstacle to be surmounted, but a growth step in the education of teachers; the evaluation is a procedure in which colleagues in the school participate along with the preparing institution, and perhaps other interested parties such as students and parents. For the participating teachers certification of the new practitioner is both an additional learning experience for themselves and a contribution to the growth of their profession. In-service preparation of the candidate for certification would become a part of the ongoing collaboration within the group. In such a process the candidate becomes highly self-evaluative. If teaching had by any chance been a poor vocational choice, it would become clear to the applicant long before the date of final determination; if on the other hand practice confirmed the choice of profession, the daily friendly contact with colleagues would greatly increase professional growth.

SUMMARY

We have looked at the four elements a fairly typical teacher, the Adams teacher, saw in her environment: the students, their parents, her colleagues, and her institution. The evidence relating to the teacher's own interests in respect to each of these strongly suggests the merits of active partnership.

The larger question of accounting for educational achievement which has created so much uneasiness among teachers and other educators must become a concern shared with both students and community, and a shared activity. When there are inadequacies or other problems, the appropriate action is not to single out for blame, which is logically inappropriate in the educational enterprise in any case, but to join in analysis of need. Without the artificial walls between teachers, and between teachers and other members of the school community, there is room and incentive for growth as there can never be under the present unreal conditions of isolation.

CHAPTER SIX

Students
in Equal Partnership

ADULTS HAVE BEEN EXCEEDINGLY SLOW to admit students into collaboration on equal terms. Most adults are more aware of the developmental differences between themselves and young people than they are of the significant strengths of youth. Whatever differences may be perceived, however, young people belong in the open partnership. Just as other groups bring varied expertise and talent to joint endeavor, so youth bring unique contributions in idealistic motivation, candid approach, clear perceptions of reality, and generous energies. Moreover, the same reasons obtain for legitimacy of student involvement in decisions which affect the fortune of their daily lives and futures as for other groups in the community. Whether the decision concerns a program or a rule, it is more successfully developed when those affected are involved.

The rarity with which this occurs raises serious questions about the adequacy of the process with which we bring young people to adulthood, about the inadequacies of the present adult-youth relationships, and for the outcome of these inadequacies in the quality of the next generation. Indeed, what is commonly described as "the crisis in school discipline,"[1] the degree to which adult-student re-

[1]*Discipline Crisis in Schools: The Problem, Causes, and Search for Solutions*, National School Public Relations Association, Arlington, Va., 1973.

lationships have deteriorated in many school systems, suggests strongly that where this occurs, neither adults nor students have much faith in the quality of available education.

One could wish that the slow progress of recent years in accepting student participation had come more widely from recognition of its educational advantages. Reality urges, however, that a much greater stimulus has been the action of the courts on the constitutional rights of students as persons.

Student efforts to determine their own interests, or to assert their own views about educational decisions which concern their interests, were generally rejected until student antiwar protests in the 1960s forced public attention and initiated court cases. The landmark decision of the U.S. Supreme Court on *Tinker v. Des Moines Independent Community School District* in February 1969, which allowed students to express antiwar views, was first of a growing body of court decisions which are still delineating the legal rights of students.

School administrators widely reacted with alarm. Subsequent studies by various secondary school principals' associations and other observers did not find the decisions onerous or overrestrictive of appropriate discretionary powers. Many school systems use procedures approximating those prescribed by the Supreme Court, such as the suspension procedures discussed in *Goss v. Lopez*. A number of educators have pointed out that fair and responsible treatment of students as required by the Supreme Court decision has always been sound practice.[2]

Nevertheless large numbers of administrators continue to find the changing status of students as persons with constitutional rights a new and irritating complication in what they see as problems of control. One state principals' association published an official review of the 1973 decisions on such problems as locker searches, distribution of literature, dress codes, and disciplinary hearings which concluded that "for the most part, the courts without abandoning the emphasis on individual constitutional rights of students, have

[2]Cf. Ronald J. Anson, "The Educator's Response to *Goss* and *Wood*," *Phi Delta Kappan*, September 1975.

broadened the authority of school officials."[3] Yet at the same time the association formally opposed a "student rights and responsibilities" bill drawn by the state student advisory council to codify pertinent court decisions, even though the bill was filed and supported by the state board of education.

High school administrators regarded the Vietnam-inspired legislation to enfranchise eighteen-year-olds as a serious threat because of the disruption of requirements for parental permission for absence from school, participation in athletics, handling report cards, attendance on field trips, and other school matters.[4] In one state similarly inspired legislation to reduce the "drinking age" to eighteen brought heated opposition from the administrative associations. Although abuse of alcohol had forced cancellation of major social events in most high schools, the issue was made an issue of control rather than a question of the poor state of existing alcohol education. Most students, therefore, were led to regard the use of drugs, including alcohol, as a "rights" controversy in an adversary situation rather than a matter of personal values and health education.

All these situations and numerous others are seen as problems of control. Comparatively seldom are differences of view in a school community treated as shared problems, in the solution of which student involvement might become equivalent to what adults call responsible citizenship in an adult society. Comparatively seldom is the school regarded as a community; rather it is regarded as an institution in which adults are responsible for students under the old precept of *in loco parentis*, with the emphasis on assumption of parental authority rather than parental concern. For students, on the other hand, the expected definition of responsibility is obedience, the hierarchic norm. Because there is an obvious conflict between the legal and cognitive recognition of students as people with individual rights and the educator's concept of students as children to care for and "educate," there is an increasing feeling among both teachers and administrators of being caught in a new and confusing situation.

[3] *The MSSPA Bugle*, Massachusetts Secondary School Principals Association, November 1973.
[4] *Education U.S.A.*, Jan. 21, 1974, p. 109.

DISCIPLINE AND EDUCATION

Most educators see discipline as a primary goal, a means for teaching and learning, achieved through maintenance of controls, rather than a developmental process which is part of learning. In this perception the general public largely supports the educators. Many adults see behavioral problems as paramount in relationships with the young and therefore see discipline as a primary goal of education.[5]

The public has been inclined to lay this responsibility on schools because it has become economically and socially convenient to keep young people separated in an artificially long maturation process. The conditions of the process do not allow for natural growth into adulthood. That is, regulations are seldom mutually agreed upon by students and adults, so that students in most schools are always chafing somewhat at rules they feel appropriate to people younger than they.

In addition, the general public has fostered school management which deals with students in numbers. Most administrators and many teachers think of students in numbers rather than as individuals. Thus from the hierarchic point of view one problem in permitting students to make more of their own decisions is simply a problem of mass. Decision sharing requires attention to individuals. The notion of a mass of individuals is threatening, and more of a challenge to professional abilities than many school people feel able to sustain. As a situation becomes difficult, there is a tendency to confuse controls with discretionary judgments involved in the educational process. The less there is of personal contact, the more arbitrary the decisions applied are likely to be.

Decision sharing on any level sometimes involves emotional problems; between adults and students reluctance is compounded by the underlying classic threat of young to old. Adult pride is involved in many cases, and apprehension for one's ability to maintain status. Therefore, whatever means for participation in school governance may be requested—student council, ad hoc committee, allowing student representatives to speak on matters of passing interest, or even

---

[5]Cf. George H. Gallup, "Seventh Annual Gallup Poll of Public Attitudes toward Education," *Phi Delta Kappan*, December 1975, pp. 227–241.

provision for student choice of major courses—a common reaction among educators is defensive and rejecting.

A poignant instance is described in a film called *Someone Has to Listen* which was based on an incident in one of the Charlotte–Mecklenburg high schools in North Carolina. An interrracial group of friends among the students developed a plan to deal with unrest arising from desegregation of their school through an "activities period" which would help the students to know one another by working together. The students were repeatedly put off from any serious discussion of their proposals, until the principal's invariable response, "Well, I'll have to think about this . . . " became a byword. Feelings grew bitter among the students generally and incidents multiplied, until one incident triggered a minor riot. Afterward the group of students began over again. In the final scene the principal started to say as usual, "Well, I'll have to think about this . . ," and stopped. He said, "Let's hear about your plans."[6]

The incident is typical of the manner in which most schools are bending young twigs without considering very much where the trees will incline. That is, they concentrate on smooth management without considering the consequences of passive behavior on the part of students on their future capacity for decision making and adult responsibility.

A striking example of these consequences is found in the Westin survey of almost seven thousand junior and senior high school students in the greater New York and Philadelphia areas over a twenty-one-month period in the late 1960s. Students were interviewed in regular social studies classes; that is, the students interviewed were not preselected, and administrators and teachers accepted the project's purposes.

Students were given a form with the following question:

Sometimes a group has trouble being as democratic as its members would like it to be. Sometimes a person is not sure what is the democratic thing to do. Other times it seems as if no one can

---

[6]*Someone Has to Listen*, film produced by the Charlotte–Mecklenburg, N.C., Public Schools for National PTA, 1973.

change the way things are enough to make a democracy work in a place like a school or a town. When someone wants to do new things or do things in a new way, it can start a fuss. Please write about one time when something like this happened to you or you saw something like this happen in your group or your school.[7]

The students were then asked to indicate "which of our names for problems in democratic behavior" fitted the story best: dissent, equality, decision making, or due process.

One student related a discussion between interested students and the new superintendent, who responded to a question that he would not hesitate to search a student's locker if he felt illegal drugs were there and that if he found drugs he would confiscate them and call the police. The students argued that such action would violate their constitutional rights, and they departed unconvinced to the contrary. The student telling the story felt that it was an instance of arbitrary action on the part of the adult. An observer could feel that a potential learning situation had been allowed to become a confrontation, and the superintendent lost an opportunity for guiding the students through the problem of handling a complex set of responsibilities.[8]

The report says that this story was unusual for raising more than a personal issue. Overall, however, the reaction of the students in relating their stories showed certain common feelings:

A large majority of the students feel they are regularly subjected to undemocratic decisions. These are seen as unilateral actions by teachers and administrators that deny fundamental rights of persons to equality, dissent, or due process, and of members of an institution to some meaningful share in its rule-making processes. Students feel that the results of the dilemma situations are bad, and report increased levels of dissatisfaction, tension, frustration, and anger with school as a result of the outcomes. Because they cannot see ways to resolve their dilemmas through

[7]Alan F. Westin and Deann Murphy, *Civic Education in a Crisis Age: An Alternative to Repression and Revolution*, Summary of a Research Project to Develop Objectives for a New Civic Education Curriculum for American Secondary Schools in the 1970s, Columbia University and Teachers College, New York, September 1970, p. 17.

[8]Ibid., p. 9.

the use of alternative means, they register strong feelings of powerlessness. . . .[9]

More than 80 percent of the students offered no alternative solutions to their dilemmas. Less than 20 percent of the respondents felt they had any options, and these largely by "conviction" that options must be possible. The students overwhelmingly accepted unilateral decision by authorities as the only available means of resolving a conflict. Less than 17 percent mentioned "talking things over," which could be defined as negotiation. Less than 20 percent of the conflict incidents were resolved by force, and over half of these involved use of force by authorities against subordinates. Very few suggested force by subordinates against authorities.

The participating students included a broad mix of socio-economic status, race, religion, and nationality. Their schools were lower class and middle class, urban and suburban, with one school for gifted students. Dissatisfaction was greater among high school than among junior high school students, but, significantly, there was no evidence of developmental change in the ability to see alternatives for action between junior high and high school students. There were no differences in use of force between suburban and urban schools. Suburban students mentioned school governance issues more often, and also more unilateral decision making by authorities, whereas urban students described more equality and due-process incidents, and more conflict resolution through force. There were differences among schools with predominantly black or predominantly white students, but not between predominantly black schools and predominantly white schools.[10]

The feelings of the students represented in the Westin and Murphy survey have been borne out by other surveys in different parts of the country. Buxton and Prichard found that 81 percent of 815 students in three high schools, urban, suburban, and rural, in three southern states, perceived "teachers to be violating the right to re-

[9]Ibid., pp. 1–2.
[10]Ibid., pp. 10–12.

spect for their [the students'] opinions.'' These student comments were typical:

> A teacher of mine thinks she is always the one that's right; she never gives another person the right to explain himself. . . . One feeling seems to dominate the administration's policy toward students—fear. The attitude seems to be "nip it in the bud,'' but there's no attempt to discover if it is a weed or a rose. . . . Students don't learn; they are simply told what to do.[11]

In a *Life* magazine survey more than 60 percent of the students polled in one hundred high schools across the country wanted more involvement in making rules and deciding curriculum, whereas only 20 percent of the parents and 35 percent of the teachers felt students should have more participation.[12]

To the students public school represents adult society. They are led to expect that the behavior they learn in schools will be appropriate for adulthood. The evidence of the Westin and Murphy survey is that most students are not in the habit of conceiving or are unable to conceive alternatives for unsatisfactory solutions, and that they either do not or are unable to perceive strength in group action. Further, a strong emphasis on self-interest appeared in many responses. Such evidence is easily related to that widespread national malaise called "don't get involved.''

Concurring evidence appears in the disappointing findings of the National Assessment of Educational Progress (NAEP) in the survey on citizenship education. Less than half of seventeen-year-olds and of young adults knew how to use a ballot, and large numbers were unaware that civil rights are constitutional rights. Political knowledge and aptitudes ran substantially below the expectations of the NAEP panel.[13]

---

[11]Thomas H. Buxton and Keith W. Prichard, "Student Perceptions of Teacher Violation of Human Rights,'' *Phi Delta Kappan*, September 1973, pp. 66–69.

[12]LIFE Poll conducted by Louis Harris, *Life*, May 16, 1969, pp. 24–25.

[13]*NAEP Newsletter*, Education Commission of the States, Denver, December 1973.

When eighteen-year-olds came into the suffrage, the student vote was not larger proportionately than the over-twenty-one vote. There were scattered youth candidates, but no reported impact to bear out predictions of either proponents or opponents of the under-twenty-one vote. In 1974 the Association of Secondary School Principals published survey findings under the headline, "Today's Students Are Straight Arrow." The survey found that a majority of two thousand young people interviewed in a national probability sample said that "they were sold on the worth of their high school education, plan to graduate and are tending to take on their parents' views regarding jobs, politics, and school. . . . Interest in politics is practically zero (1%) among today's high school students . . . and only one in ten stated a willingness to run for elective office."[14]

Such findings are the more disappointing to citizenship educators in that substantial innovations have expanded the one-time "civics" classes. After a CBS National Citizenship Test several years ago brought "excellent" scores from only 10 percent of a major national audience, and a "poor" score from 61 percent, teachers began taking their classes into municipal meetings, courtrooms, and political campaigns in an effort to show how the adult community operates. The national phenomenon known as Watergate brought another resurgence in civic education. A northeastern states regional convention for teachers focused on questions which Watergate raised for the classroom. If the resolutions which the convention adopted are indicative, however, and if subsequent publications for teachers' use are indicative, education for citizenship still concerns itself with what goes on outside the school rather than in students' own lives.[15]

The NAEP survey found a high percentage of democratic attitudes among students—higher than expected, in fact; but the understanding necessary to carry such attitudes into practice was lacking.

[14]*Education U.S.A.*, Mar. 11, 1974, p. 153.
[15]E.g., *It Starts in the Classroom*, National School Public Relations Association, Arlington, Va., January 1974. All thirteen instances of exemplary teaching about Watergate pertained to Watergate itself.

The evidence of the survey was that classroom discussions and political fieldwork, however interesting, will not of themselves develop responsible citizens. Rather, from what students say of their schools as political environment, one must conclude that if students are to learn in school the habits of adult responsibility, only the habit and expectation of participation in decisions of actual moment to the participant can be effective education for adult citizenship.

Being able to participate in decision making that matters is equivalent to being treated as an equal, something to which every one of us is exceedingly sensitive—young people as much as any. This is the nub of the schools' dilemma. Schools are a hierarchic system, whose practicing definition of responsibility is obedience. The teachers and administrators who treat young people with honest respect as equals, who offer partnership in learning and attempt to guide young people into adult initiatives, are still regarded as more or less deviant. The expectation of conformity is the basis of school management, and conformity is incompatible with equality.

We should be deeply concerned with what students are telling us of their distrust. Skepticism is not an atmosphere for learning. The distrust students feel must inevitably bear upon learning achievement. Moreover, at least as disturbing in its implications for all of us, this kind of education is not education for democracy.

TEACHING FOR VIOLENCE

Conformity is not providing the desired peace in the schools. Violence and vandalism are becoming more prominent in the public eye than education itself. Rather than stimulating examination of the system, however, its problems are met by demands for more conformity, until current programs of "school security" commonly utilize both highly technical electronic equipment and uniformed police in school corridors and classrooms.

School administrators, and indeed many observers, tend to divide students between the troublesome and the nontroublesome, between the sheep and the goats. "Probably no more than 10 percent of the school population is felt to be responsible for the violence and vandalism now recorded in schools,'' says a current handbook for parents.[16] Therefore, it is said, control of the 10 percent will itself solve the problems of vandalism and other violence and allow peaceful education of the 90 percent.

It is far too little understood that the kind of school-student relationship seen in the Westin and Murphy survey prevails in most schools, even in schools where a benevolent climate seems to prevail. As Westin pointed out,

> Some observers may have been inclined to brush aside recent secondary school demonstrations and protests as the work of a few radical agitators. . . . But our survey suggests that the great majority of students in secondary schools—the supposedly "silent majority"—is becoming increasingly frustrated and alienated by school. They do not believe that they receive individual justice or enjoy the right to dissent, or share in critical rule-making that affects their lives.[17]

It is also far too little understood that if students have no experience of resolving differences democratically, or of initiating alternatives and participating in the decisions, in these formative years, the great majority of them are being educated either for conformity or for violence in dealing with problems in adulthood. Rollo May comments on the efforts of psychologists to rid children of aggressive tendencies, and his comments apply to other measures taken in schools to secure docility:

> What is *not* seen is that the state of powerlessness, which leads to apathy and which can be produced by the above plans for the uprooting of aggression, is the source of violence. As we make people powerless, we promote their violence rather than its control. Deeds of violence in our society are performed largely by those trying to establish their self-esteem, to defend their self-image, and to demonstrate that they, too, are significant.[18]

[16]*Violence in Our Schools: What to Know about It—What to Do about It*, National Committee for Citizens in Education, Columbia, Md., 1975, p. 6.

[17]Westin and Murphy, op. cit., p. 2.

[18]Rollo May, *Power and Innocence*, Norton, New York, 1972, p. 23.

The methods of control used in schools have become bitter issues among those concerned for the rights of students, whether the methods used are unilateral decision, corporal punishment, classroom manipulation, or drugs to control "hyperactive" students. Each denigrates the individual and leaves lasting scars, simply to make an adult task easier. Indeed, a great many arbitrary actions taken by adults, parents as well as teachers, are taken simply to be rid of a situation rather than to find a solution. Teachers who depend on controls to any degree inevitably tend to depend proportionately less upon their educational skills; thus not only are they not using their skills to best advantage, but if controls fail they find themselves at a disadvantage. Take, for instance, this eighth-grade youngster in a Visalia, California, school. His teachers found him frightening. He was only fourteen, but weighed 185 pounds; he was easily the school's best athlete, but loved fighting even more than he loved sports. He had knocked other students out "cold" with beer bottles and chairs. Hitting the principal with a stick had cost him a forty-day suspension, arrest, and a 2½-year probation for assault. Finally he was assigned to a special education teacher who helped his troubled junior high school students cope with their problems by teaching them "behavior engineering." That is, he taught them to deal with teachers and peers by reinforcing with smiles and approval the behavior they liked and ignoring the behavior they disliked:

> His math teacher was one of the first to encounter his new techniques. Jess asked for help with a problem, and when she had finished her explanation, he looked her in the eye and said, "You really help me learn when you're nice to me." The startled teacher groped for words, and then said, "You caught on quickly." Jess smiled, "It makes me feel good when you praise me."[19]

Here was a transferable technique which ameliorated a difficult situation, considerably more effective than efforts to "discipline" or control a very independent and physically effective youngster. The

[19]Farnum Gray with Paul S. Graubard and Harry Rosenberg, "Little Brother Is Changing You," *Psychology Today*, March 1974, p. 42 ff.

method placed him in a position of equality, a point which might disturb those who are convinced of the need for "professional" control; but the student's basic goal was learning, and that was the way he used his new skill. When more educators learn that the feeling of equality encourages learning, and that their own teaching skills are more effective in this context, one likely outcome is more peace in our classrooms.

The system of hierarchic controls has sometimes led to arbitrary action and reaction which itself teaches violence to young people. In the history of the long and painful decade before the Boston schools were desegregated by federal court order, there can be identified various steps to school disruption. One of these incidents seems to have triggered open student protest for the first time. One morning in September 1968 two students wore dashikis to English High School, where the dress code required coat and tie, and were promptly suspended. A confusion of parent protest, affirmation, countermanding, and reaffirmation of the order followed, during which white students demanded an equal right to go without ties. The school committee reluctantly agreed to receive a student delegation, heard the brief student presentation (which was televised) with obvious coolness, and rejected the delegation's requests. The students responded, black and white, with protests and boycotts which spread to other schools across the city and resulted in hundreds of rollicking boys and girls marching in the streets. At this point the school committee gave in—a lesson in civic action which was not lost on the students. The underlying issue was not the wearing of dashikis or ties; it was the long-standing poor quality of education and the arbitrary nature of the structure of school governance, both of which had long since developed unrest. Up to that point, however, only adults had held protest demonstrations, which were largely contained. It took the backing down of the chief school authority to teach the students that violence succeeds where argument fails.

Here and elsewhere, almost of necessity, schools countered student activism with police action, and the period of student protest and demonstration largely passed into a period of covert vandalism and random violence. Schools used even more liberally the measures of suspension and expulsion, until court cases began to result in due process requirements. General opposition to suspension and violence increased in the growing conviction that both are counterproductive to education and in most cases serve other than student interests.

When the Boston school department turned to the standard remedy and proposed to send the "known troublemakers" to school on a harbor island, U.S. District Judge W. Arthur Garrity, Jr., under whose jurisdiction the schools now operated, refused permission, saying the students were "entitled to go to school. They can't be sent to an educational Siberia just because they are aggressive." He said that aggressive students are often the future leaders of the community, and that "these may be the ones who would most benefit from a normal education."[20]

As to vandalism, the wide spectrum of measures which schools have been taking range from heavy electronic security and strictly imposed controls on students to more attentive study of the school environment and involvement of students in solving the common problems. At one extreme are schools such as Wyandanch High School, Long Island, New York, where the principal has brought previous violence under control through highly organized and inflexible curriculum, firm and consistent discipline, swift punishment of infractions, and removal of "chronic troublemakers" to an "adjustment program." Activity programs are encouraged, writes a Wyandanch teacher, and students are quoted as "happier with guidance, direction, and authority." The picture is reminiscent of *Walden Two*.[21] in that "habits are being formed that will serve Wyandanch students in years to come." But has vandalism been cured? According to the teacher, "The answer is no. Peace in the schools is maintained by eternal vigilance."[22]

A different view has been offered by a study of the issues

[20]William J. Doherty, Courtesy of the *Boston Globe*, Oct. 30, 1975.

[21]B.F. Skinner, *Walden Two*, Macmillan, New York, 1962.

[22]Joseph Wint, "Contrasting Solutions for School Violence: 1. The Crackdown," *Phi Delta Kappan*, November 1975, pp. 175–176.

surrounding vandalism made by the Harvard Architectural Research Office. The study found that only about half of the property damage commonly called vandalism is the result of violent and malicious acts; other damage is the result of "rough play, inadequate initial school planning, and the pragmatic solutions students work out to satisfy their legitimate needs to gather and to play." The study urges better design, more responsive to student needs, without resort to "prison-like" alternatives, together with programs of education and dialogue.[23]

Toward the other end of the spectrum, also, schools are finding that getting students involved in prevention of violence is a key point in solving the problem. In one New England high school parking lot thefts were ended almost completely when patrol duties were turned over to the students.[24] Students in the Martin Luther King Elementary School in Portland, Oregon, started an antivandalism campaign that reduced vandalism in their own school to near zero and then carried the ideas to other schools through workshops, essay contests, drama skits, and other creative methods. The Portland school board credited these students with a large part in dropping vandalism costs in the city schools from $70,000 to $60,000 in two years.[25]

The Harvard study cites high schools in South San Francisco, California, and in Shrewsbury, Massachusetts, where the repair budgets were given to high school students to manage; the balance remaining in the second semester became available to a worthwhile project. The objectives were to educate students as to the cost of vandalism, such as relating the cost of twenty broken windows to the cost of a new projector, and to the enjoyment of the positive advantages of making repairs unnecessary. It was noticed that vandalism of student group projects stopped almost immediately, and it was hoped

[23]*Analysis to Reduce Property Damage*, Harvard University, Graduate School of Design, Architectural Research Office, Massachusetts Advisory Council on Education, Boston, 1975.

[24]*Education U.S.A.*, Jan. 13, 1975, p. 111.

[25]The Honorable Robert Packwood, "Elementary Schools' Program for Reducing Vandalism Shows Results," *Congressional Record*, Apr. 27, 1970, S6227.

that this partnership attitude would carry over to the entire building and grounds.

The simplest method of controlling vandalism, curiously enough, seems to be called upon only in random instances: the active presence of parents in the schools. Parents are in the school in numbers generally where vandalism is not a problem, and therefore the connection may have gone unremarked, or in places where the situation has deteriorated to the extent that parents have insisted upon intervention. This intervention has occurred successfully in some Boston junior high schools.

When we can realize that vandalism is the expression of anger and frustration and powerlessness, we can begin to focus on the nub of the problem: the student's own view of himself or herself and the resulting relationship between student and school. It is often a matter of accident and personality whether frustration and anger are expressed in restlessness or in drug use or in some act of violence. All of these are symptoms of relationship problems. A student who commits a crime must be punished in some appropriate manner, but school and family must share in the sense of failure. The chance of avoiding student crime is considerably better if parents are also sharing in the process of education—if education is visibly a three-way partnership. Parents in the schools, whether in the corridors—a successful measure in some city schools—or in classrooms, clinic, library, or whatever, give students a better sense of belonging. Contrary to the administrative myth, this is just as true for high schools as for elementary schools. One of the traumas of adolescence is the separation from families forced both by schools and (perhaps this is related) by peer society. The youngsters who have the easiest maturation are those who stay in communication with their families. The all but universal acceptance of the educators' edict that parents are not wanted in schools creates grave difficulties for parents in maintaining communication with their young people and for young people in maintaining a sense of belonging.

If adults want the next generation to become confident individuals who respect themselves, are willing to obey laws, value the rights of others, and forgo private gain at public expense, we must recognize that young people must be allowed to grow up in close working arrangements with adults and to be involved in determining their own lives, whatever the inconvenience and whatever the "professional" dogmas that are offended. If young people do not learn the democratic arts of decision making and self-disciplined responsibility in their formative years, it is a matter of chance whether they do so later.

SIGNS OF CHANGE

The arts of sharing decisions seem to be easier for students to accept than for adults to learn. Young people are realistic. They are perceptive of the limits and possibilities of a situation, and make good use of an actual opportunity. Despite a generally uneasy situation, there are many records of successful involvement.

For instance, it is well known that student councils have been held in small regard among students because the councils have so seldom been allowed to deal with problems that mattered to the students. In 1972 student advisory councils came to be required by law in Massachusetts. The legislation was enacted through the strong support of the commissioner of education, the education department staff, the governor, legislators, and students, rather than through efforts of local school or community people. The students proceeded over the next two years to use their new opportunities effectively; they developed a communication network, held workshops and training programs, and established relationships with other school organizations. Through action of the councils and their representatives in the regional and state councils, they developed a sizable legislative program each year which dealt with student rights and responsibilities, curriculum innovation, privileged communication between students and school personnel, and student involvement on local school committees. Council representatives negotiated support for much of their legislation from other school organizations and legislators. Another law enabled the state student advisory council to elect a member to the state board of education who is regarded not as a "student member" but a member in full standing.

As long ago as 1969 the school board of Burlington, Vermont, invited the high school students to elect four seniors to a search committee for a new superintendent of schools. The student reaction was enthusiastic, an election was immediately arranged, and the student representatives had equal status with the committee's adult members.[26]

The California Association of Student Councils recommends student membership on school boards, student involvement in budget and program planning, and, so far as is possible, equal student-adult membership on joint committees. "The basic problem in dealing with students," it is added, "is the adults' tendency to want conformity in them despite the fact that each of us differs from the next. . . . . Students must be convinced that involvement will be worth while for them. To do this, administrators will have to counteract their reputation of listening to students only for listening's sake."[27]

This statement represents one of the myriad ways young people point out that schools must deal with the basic problems of respect for individuals before they can deal with the question of decision sharing. This requirement applies whether school authorities are dealing with a student council or adult members are working with students in a representative council. One student reported that she felt the advisory council she belonged to at the Bronx High School of Science ought to be reorganized to comprise five students and a total of five parents and teachers, instead of five students, five parents, and five faculty members, because "the votes are almost always ten to five." Even so, she admitted that "the students still get a great deal said," and the adults reported that they now had a chance to voice their own grievances in front of the students.[28]

The National School Boards Association held a clinic on "How

[26]Reprinted by permission from the *Christian Science Monitor*, Jan. 16, 1969. © The Christian Science Publishing Society. All rights reserved.

[27]Bruce Lymburn, California Association of Student Councils, "Recommendations for Student Involvement," *Education for the People*, vol. 2, a Resource Book for School-Community Decision Making, Education Resources Center, San Mateo County, Calif., 1971.

[28]Landt Dennis, reprinted by permission from *Christian Science Monitor*, Sept. 4, 1971, © The Christian Science Publishing Society. All rights reserved.

to Involve Students in Decision-Making" with the following program descriptor: "Honest, good-faith efforts to involve students in decision-making is what the experts call insurance against student unrest."

"I reject that assumption," said Dean Young, one of the participants. "Our efforts should be directed toward utilizing the potential that student unrest represents, not toward destroying it. . . . If you don't truly believe that students possess the competence and the legitimate right for that kind of involvement you will not fool the students by professing that you do."[29]

One encouragement to admitting students into decision making is to utilize the indubitable talents young people have for problem solving. Young describes an incident in which the student advisory council of a high school complained to the superintendent of a long-standing problem with the study halls and the library, both overcrowded, which were used for socializing as much as for study and were therefore noisy. The superintendent said the problem required study. The students responded with a floor plan of the high school, a room usage chart, analysis of use, and a new schedule.

The year after graduation some Hingham High School (Massachusetts) graduates returned to tell administrators that the opportunity for independence they found in college was far more conducive to good work, and that one could tell which college students had learned to be independent. Their point: Was it really necessary to "spoon-feed" high school students? The administration agreed to offer options of using study halls (without teachers present) where students would allow no talking so that they could concentrate, or the cafeteria where arguments could flourish, or small rooms for cooperative projects. The plan worked, with very few losses of privilege, and the teachers were delighted with the opportunity to get on with other work. Thereafter students were allowed to plan their own assemblies and sports functions, and one administrator admitted that even "school spirit" was coming back.[30]

[29]Dean A. Young, "A Legitimate Right," *MASC Journal*, Massachusetts Association of School Committees, March 1973. Reprinted from *Ohio School Boards Association Journal*.

[30]Phyllis W. Coons, Courtesy of the *Boston Globe*, Dec. 29, 1968.

The principal of the Salmon, Idaho, high school accepted a student offer proposing that the school board set aside $500 to cover window breakage and let the students have whatever was left to buy a gift for the school, because "they thought a self-policing plan would work." Broken windows that year had cost more than $2,000. The following year the total was about $30, mainly from accidental damage.[31]

Effective involvement is not limited to high schools. A Cleveland elementary teacher described "a representative council of parents, teachers, and our own children. . . . We've allowed the children to initiate the discussions. They're concerned with why they can't have a lunch program, why they can't use the school in the evenings, and one question—the kids raise this—is: What are parents doing to improve the behavior of our children?"[32]

A great many PTAs have become PTSAs, or parent-teacher-student associations. These are not only high school groups, but junior high and middle, elementary, and even primary school groups, in which students hold equal membership and serve as committee members and officers. The National PTA Board of Managers includes five student members between the ages of fifteen and twenty, and six of the state branches are PTSAs. With PTA as representative of the country as a whole as it is, it is not surprising that student membership is not universally welcomed; nevertheless student membership has increased steadily and PTSAs tend to be more consistently active groups.

STUDENTS ARE PEOPLE

"If you wonder how to avoid violating students' rights while maintaining discipline in the classroom," advised one teacher, "treat each student, regardless of age, as you would an adult, and solid rapport is in the offing."[33]

[31]*Boston Globe*, Feb. 9, 1969, Associated Press.

[32]Alfred Aiello, John W. Raper Elementary School, Cleveland, quoted in Philip Sterling (ed.), *The Real Teachers*, Random House, New York, 1972, p. 85. Copyright, Random House, 1972.

[33]*It Starts in the Classroom*, National School Public Relations Association, Arlington, Va., January 1975.

A variety of influences is undoubtedly bringing educators to free themselves from the felt necessity of treating children and young people as inferiors, and to view their interaction with students in a more personal light. Among such influences are the repeated documentations of the "Pygmalion" effect, with not only the positive effects of high expectations but the serious implications of the dampening effects of negative expectations, the growing social skills of students and their parents, and the increasing consciousness of teachers' own accountability.

Bilingual programs are another influence, a concept itself progressing through stages of understanding. The teachers who have for many years been teaching Spanish-speaking first graders without knowing a word of Spanish, and there are many, are now being asked to understand the weight of guilt placed upon the youngster who is forced to speak English or fail. Haskins rightly asked:

> Is there any real attitudinal difference between making Mexican American children kneel and ask forgiveness if discovered speaking their native language in school and the description of a new bilingual program by a Massachusetts educator as "*we* will allow them to speak Spanish *until* they learn English"?[34]

It took strong advocacy forces to bring about the change from illegality to legality of minority languages in American public schools. Unless schools respond with collaborative efforts, the adversary effect of advocacy will color school-community and inter-community relationships. Such questions as Haskins' help to encourage change in underlying attitudes and the gradual acceptance of bicultural as well as bilingual education.

Inter-grade-level tutoring is another program which enhances both self-esteem and learning, and this also came from efforts to meet a special need. It began with an experimental program in delinquency prevention in 1967 undertaken by Judge Mary Conway Kohler and a newly formed National Commission on Resources for

---

[34]Kenneth W. Haskins, "Implications: New Conceptions of Relevancy," *Educational Leadership*, May 1972, p. 688.

Youth. Not all the schools which copied the idea understood its basic intent. Whereas some schools reward their high-achieving students with tutoring roles, the original tutors were underachievers. Of the two hundred tutors teaching four hundred students in Newark and Philadelphia during the summer of 1967, the tutors in Newark, for example, gained on standard tests an average of three years and five months in reading levels.[35] Alexander Mood later commented about the program, "When a student has difficulty with an idea, give him the task of teaching it to a couple of younger children and he will pore over it mightily."[36] On the other hand, Mood recommended rotating all students into teaching roles, and this has advantages. As the perceptive principal of Colebrook said of the quicker sixth-graders assigned to tutoring, "They expect instant learning," and themselves begin to learn something of differences in people. A high school student said, "You don't realize the problems teachers have until you try tutoring." The underachiever from a higher grade level is sensitive to the learning process of the younger child and can more easily share the steps to solutions. The achievers who are assigned to tutoring, on the other hand, also have the opportunity to learn something about collaboration.

YOUNG INITIATIVES

Students need real rather than vicarious activities if they are to develop responsibility for their own actions. Activities which are suspected of artificiality or "busywork" are not taken seriously. If students participate at all, they will do so passively, so that the net influence is toward other passive behavior, such as "dreaming," or drug use.

In the conviction that society has closed off most of the old

[35]Leslie Rich, "The Magic Ingredient of Volunteerism," *American Education*, June 1973, p. 7.

[36]Alexander M. Mood, *Do Teachers Make a Difference?* paper for a conference sponsored by the Bureau of Educational Personnel Development, U.S. Office of Education, 1970.

pathways by which young people make the transition from adolescence to constructive adult life, the National Commission on Resources for Youth began "scouting the country" for examples of new programs that have overcome adult blockades to make productive participation and responsibility for young people possible. Over some five years the commission researched and documented more than eight hundred different successful student projects. They included curriculum building, student teaching, community service, archaeology, business enterprises, community problem solving, publishing and filmmaking, and resources for youth in trouble. Judge Kohler says the students are not starry-eyed:

> Youthful idealism is of course important, but that's only part of the picture. These kids have imagination. They have insight. They have more ability to size up a situation and decide what to do about it than most adults seem to realize. They need some guidance from competent adults, of course. But these kids don't want to be thought of as passive do-gooders ready to follow whatever orders someone chooses to give them. They want to participate, to be part of the action. And that means contributing ideas, taking part in the planning, making decisions, and following through, often to the extent of fully operating projects they themselves conceive of.[37]

For instance, a sixteen-year-old student in Enfield High School, Connecticut, stopped a department head in the corridor:

> Been working on an idea. Lots of cities, like New York, have a setup where they record their history on tape. Supposing we went them one better and set up a center where we preserve this town's heritage in both sight and sound—letting the kids do the job. . . .
> What does an expressway do to a community? How can we save our landmarks? What happens to a Puerto Rican if he comes here to live? So we create small teams of two or three kids and a teacher who shares a concern about something. We send them out into the field with cameras and tape recorders. They learn how to ask questions and take pictures that tell the

[37]Rich, op. cit., p. 5.

story. Then they bring the stuff back to the lab, put it together with a synchronized sound track, and we use the unit to teach the other kids what makes their town tick.[38]

This student's vision became reality, with additional innovations including student publications and the development of what the students call Lab- Carts—a compact set of shelves and equipment providing materials and methods for study of some specific topics: Indian lore, Africa, pollution, and many others. Six years later some 250 students out of 1,250 in the high school were using and operating the laboratory, had developed numbers of projects, and initiated much new curriculum. Some teachers remained skeptical, but the Lab's faculty adviser believed that the Lab had done much to ''shake students out of their reticence and insecurity'' by persuading them to try out and prove their capabilities.

A group of students in Philadelphia found their health education dull, unappealing, and ineffective for the problems they knew as immediate and pressing: drug abuse, alcoholism, venereal disease, and tuberculosis. They organized Students Concerned for Public Health and with faculty help began visiting hospitals, rehabilitation centers, and alcohol treatment agencies. Then they put together materials—a play, comic books, posters, and various puppet shows—which teams of three or four students took to the schools and playgrounds of North Philadelphia to educate younger children about health problems and health careers. The group gained recognition, adult support, and acceptance in school classrooms.

The National Commission's useful book, *New Roles for Youth in the School and the Community* (Citation Press, New York, 1974), describes these and a number of other successful projects in detail. They include youth-operated periodicals such as *Foxfire*, which originated at Rabun Gap-Nacoochee High School in Georgia and is devoted to folklore and experiences of old-timers of Appalachia, and the *Fourth Street i*, written and published by youngsters of New

---

[38]National Commission on Resources for Youth, *New Roles for Youth in the School and the Community*, Citation Press, New York, 1974, pp. 12–13.

York's lower East Side. There is a high school Indian archaeology project in Atlanta; urban renewal construction in a Denver high school; a natural science museum in Cornwall, New York; a problem-solving-action group in ecology called EARTH in the San Francisco Bay area; an Unwinding Room in Philadelphia; and an auxiliary staff at Sonoma State Hospital in northern California—among many others. All represent different approaches, as the young people involved were different, but they are alike in offering a working partnership with adults and the kind of participation that demands responsibility.

THE GROWTH OF ALTERNATIVE SCHOOLS

In the 1950s both cultural and political dissatisfactions led to the appearance of "free schools," some of which were scarcely schools. In the 1960s, however, students, teachers, parents, and administrators, in various combinations, began to turn to alternative programs in separate schools within the public school system where students could learn responsibility by having and using it.

Students organized some of the first alternative schools, seeking education they felt they had been denied in public schools. One of the earliest was Freedom School in Washington, D.C., which was created, established, and funded, between November 1967 and November 1968, by some 180 students organized as the Modern Strivers. The students raised money, employed teachers, decided the curriculum, and persuaded the board of education to accredit the courses which were given afternoons in a church across the street from Northeast High School where they were enrolled.

One alternative school accepted only students with problems: the Street Academy System of Springfield (Massachusetts) or SAS-SI. Ninety-five percent of its students were school dropouts or kick-outs; 52 percent had criminal records; 63 percent received public assistance; 93 percent had used drugs; and 3 percent were addicted to heroin. They were black, white, and Puerto Rican, sixteen to forty-three years of age, with an average age of nineteen.

The emphasis of SASSI's educational concepts was on hard work in academic and training skills acquisition (they called it an academic boot camp), the Lancastrian method of employing students to teach other students, and community service. Besides basic curriculum, the thirty-odd courses, included a working newspaper, SALT (Springfield Area Life and Times); a closed-circuit video system serving 150 low-income families; and a dance troupe. All of these also generated income for the school, although basic funding came from grants. Students were graduated when they were ready, in months or years. By June 1974, at the end of three years of existence, SASSI had graduated eighty-seven students, of whom seventy-two were enrolled in colleges or technical institutes and fifteen were placed in jobs. The school did not survive, because the city school system did not support its concepts and because SALT reported more about the city than some funding sources appreciated.

Another alternative school may be unique. Murray Road High School in Newton, Massachusetts, is an annex to Newton High School. It uses an abandoned elementary school which was offered by the superintendent to volunteer students and teachers in 1967. The school is run by teachers and students without an administrator; decisions are generally made by consensus, but when necessary by vote of the general meeting in which teachers and students each have one vote. Its students number approximately a hundred with six or seven teachers, and all graduates who wished to go to college have been accepted at a variety of colleges and universities. The school uses evaluations by both students and teachers instead of marks for each course, and the student evaluations have often been factors in college acceptance.

Alternative schools have been established in more than a thousand public school systems across the country. In many cases their fiscal position is not altogether secure, and one principal stressed that a part of his job was to teach his staff "survival techniques." Insofar as they govern themselves as a democratic "community," as most do, they have known all the growing pains of democratic organizations: goal conflicts, stumbling over trivia, communication problems, and narrow concerns. Some alternative school faculties feel they have built viable democratic communities; some are still struggling. Some have involved the general community, and there is evidence that these are among the more successful schools. Not all are open schools; when a highly traditional alternative school was established in Pasadena, a corner may have been turned from "allowing the trouble-makers to secede" to a recognition that different students learn more effectively in different environments.

Except for some of the alternative schools, student participation in general academic decision making has had far less attention than problems of study halls and dress codes. Ordinarily school people feel that students are unlikely to make curriculum choices leading to a program of academic quality. At least one well-documented study, however, speaks to the effect of student choice upon students' educational aspiration, responsibility, and satisfaction, upon teacher-student hostility, and upon academic achievement.

In this study students in one out of fourteen urban high schools were required to make all their academic choices.[39] There were no differences between students in the academic-choice school and those in the other schools in their plans to attend college, but there were significant differences in related activities such as reading college catalogs, making inquiries of college officials, and seeking information about colleges, suggesting that the plans of students in the academic-choice school would be more realistic and accurate. These students also appeared to be more committed to their academic programs, with more reasons for their choices, and more personal and carefully considered reasons. In related activities, these students were found to test significantly higher on important attitudes of responsibility.

Student satisfaction with the school was borne out by attendance, by positive comment on the teachers' abilities, and by evi-

---

[39]James McPartland et al., *Student Participation in High School Decisions: A Study of Students and Teachers in Fourteen Urban High Schools, Summary and Excerpts,* Johns Hopkins University, Center for the Study of Social Organization of Schools, Baltimore, 1971, pp. 22–24.

dence of more trust and respect between students and teachers. This was indicated, for instance, in less tension over deciding and enforcing what was to be expected from the student for a given grade. The crucial question, whether students given choices would "take the easy way out," was answered with the finding that students tended to balance their programs between demanding and less demanding programs. Not only was individual choice a substantial influence for sound academic decisions, but a larger than usual group of students became interested in academic goals and behavior. The fact of choice itself improved academic achievement.

One entry point to the feeling of equality in educational enterprise was opened unofficially among college students: student evaluation of teachers. Some elementary and secondary school teachers and administrators, however, have also recognized learning values in student evaluation. For instance, the Amherst-Pelham (Massachusetts) schools have used in elementary grades a student form asking the student to mark "yes," "no," or "?" for each of twenty-four statements. Three of these statements are:

My teacher sometimes lets me decide what I want to do.
My teacher wants me to say what I think.
My teacher lets me help make plans for the class.

The corresponding performance criterion is:

Plans and provides for involvement of all students in the learning process.[40]

Another sort of alternative in the public schools that allows the student some academic decisions is the "open campus" program, in which students develop learning programs with citizens outside of the school; these may be in business, in government, in the arts, or a myriad other established occupations. This alternative has had impetus from various conditions, such as lack of space in some high

[40]*Student Form for Teacher Evaluation*, Pace Project, Field Services Division, Department of Pupil and Program Appraisal, Montgomery County Public Schools, Maryland, May 1973.

schools, the troubles of large groups of students the public schools were patently unable to serve, a growing interest in career education, and the impatience of both educators and community people with wholly academic and cloistered education.

One finds with a feeling of irony that off-campus programs were already being used successfully some twenty years ago, and that a group of educators and architects met over a five-year period in the early 1950s to put together secondary education which included apprenticeship in the world of work, partnership of the community, and strong development of the individual. To this end all available resources of the whole community were to be part of the school. They called it the "Partnership Program" and the plan was published in 1956[41] Thereafter, it is reported, the advent of Sputnik turned the interests of educators in other directions, and only in the last few years did conditions combine to focus new attention on school-community programs.

A program such as that described in Chapter Two depends for its success on fulfillment of a formal contract between the student, the school, and the community resource, and on a joint evaluation by student, community "teacher," parent, and in-school faculty. Given adequate funding, competent coordination, and community resources, the success of a program is indicative of individual responsibility in the students. Students must make their own plans and their own accommodations with governmental, industrial, or other "faculty." Some school faculties are more willing than others to integrate the off-campus courses in the student's curriculum; some students must still "add on" the off-campus courses. Nevertheless, student competence has been such that the program has spread widely and rapidly. It is no longer a novelty, and schools of every type and size are involved. Some educators again see in the off-campus curriculum a pattern for the future, in which students are educated

[41]Archibald B. Shaw and John Lyon Reid, "The Random Falls Idea: An Educational Program and Plant for Youth and Community Growth," *School Executive*, March 1956.

partly in school buildings and partly in the community, because the partnership offers such strong possibilities for integrating students into society during the process of education.

Perhaps the success of the open-campus program suggests the efficacy of small beginnings, for in many cases these programs began with a half-dozen students. Even more, perhaps, it suggests that as with most human relationships some exposure and experience are necessary to perceive the values of collaboration with students. The possibilities for learning that would arise from student-educator relationships which more nearly utilize student competence and energy seem almost limitless. The basic need for adults, whether teachers, administrators, parents, or employers, is to relax into acceptance of young people as individuals and avoid the compulsive expectation of conformity.

Secondly, adults must learn to listen. Most listen with preconceived ideas of what they will hear, and therefore hear nothing. Even a little relaxation of the felt need to control, a little redressing of the balance of acceptance, would in most cases go a long way.

And finally, adults must deal honestly with children and young people. Mutual trust between teachers and students, as between parent and child, is the most important ingredient of education. As adults open doors on opportunities and accept young ideas, they must expect frequently to join with young people in working out those ideas as partners, and take seriously the product of their joint endeavors. Trust grows out of mutual confidence in being treated fairly; in either schools or families, growth builds on trust.

CHAPTER SEVEN

The Community
in Partnership

IT WOULD BE HARD TO FIND in nature an analogy for the ambivalent relationship that exists between most schools and their communities, or anything more paradoxical than the climate of uneasiness which generally pervades their communications.

Schools are the center of this generation's concern for the next generation. Families build their lives around schools. Most school decisions are taken in the name of the community and on the assumption that the community will approve. Yet the walls between school and community are such that, in all good will, parents and teachers are literally and painfully timid of one another. Parents are generally uncomfortable in school even while they are supportive and anxious to understand what is going on with their children. Teachers, on the other hand, are uncomfortable about discussing children with parents, and tend to reject any information that might sound like advice, among other reasons for the possibility that it may reflect upon their professional competence. Parents worry about schools' neglect of children's needs. Schools blame parents for lack of interest, restricted curriculum, and undisciplined youngsters. All too seldom do parents presume to suggest, or teachers admit, that "*we* share a common concern."

At the same time, the school administrator at any level is continually reminded that school programs proceed at the sufferance of the public "out there," that taxpayers are watching the budget, and that "the parents" won't like changes they don't understand. The talk of superintendents is sometimes reminiscent of the actor looking out over the footlights:

> *A big black giant who looks and listens*
> *With thousands of eyes and ears . . .*
> *Will sit out there and rule your life*
> *For all your living years.* [1]

There is something of an issue in how community is defined in relation to schools. Many school people draw a circle around the school board, administrators, faculty, staff, and students. This is the school's operation; this is the community of the school. But if we see the education of students as the focal point, the school's community comprises the students it serves and all those upon whom the quality of that education depends, in a series of concentric circles. In a larger sense the school also serves the total community through its role in preparing the next generation.

Thus citizens have varying interests as to what happens in schools. Some, particularly parents, are so closely concerned as to want a voice in curriculum and in governance; others are content to vote yes or no on bond issues according to their views of fiscal needs. Still others are concerned with education priorities from their sense of social needs. They all have a varying influence on the quality of education, according to the quality and objectives of their involvement.

Those in the innermost of these concentric circles may or may not define the school community broadly, depending on their views of mutual responsibilities between school and community; whether they readily countenance the sharing of some elements of the decision-making process of school operation depends on a complex set of personal commitments and reactions. Whatever their views may be, it is decidedly in the interests of schools to involve community people freely according to their concerns, and essential in children's interests that parents and other citizens involve themselves in effective and friendly ways, whether or not an invitation is offered.

THE CURRENT SEPARATISM

Community involvement tends to be a one-sided affair. That is, the school authorities decide how much involvement is to be accepted. Aides, funds for playground equipment or technology, participation in report-card committees, support for school bond issues—such assistance is welcomed in many schools, though, surprising as it may seem, not in all schools. Few schools welcome parents as visitors; most parents are dependent on formal parent-teacher conferences for information about their children, and these vary widely as satisfactory communication. Many parents offer help as volunteers and thus learn something of what goes on with their children; but many schools do not accept volunteers and some schools do not accept parents as volunteers where they have children.

Direct school communication to parents (other than the call from the principal's office) or to the general public is categorically regarded as a public relations program. Although considerable investments are made in public relations programs, they seldom address expressed parent or taxpayer concerns in a way that could be described as two-way communication. The broader community quite generally is dependent upon public media and gossip, and tends to be poorly informed about schools. In larger communities, moreover, the circles of actual involvement tend to become narrower, and school governance procedures more rigid.

In most schools the professional line is clearly drawn in respect to determining what or how a child is taught, how available funds are to be allocated, and who shall be employed to teach. Decision making is reserved to school boards and their administrators. The central issue of most controversy about community participation in school governance is whether or not decision making on matters of citizen concern is to be shared with interested citizens. For the most part communities take exclusion quietly, but upon occasion an outburst of resentment occurs, all the more heated for having been previously repressed: a Kanahwa County book-burning, school levies voted down, a school board election upset, a school administrator's tenure made impossible—none of which solves the underlying problems. The issue is sharper in cities where the grievances are so much greater, but suburbs and rural areas have the same problems of alienation more subtly drawn.

The chief result of excluding the community is perpetuation of the alienation itself. This may result in militance, as one or another group rebels against its feeling of powerlessness, and occasionally this militance is exploited and prolonged by opportunistic leadership. The more dangerous outcome, however, is the very acquiescence and apathy which seem to concern school people least. Apathy tends to develop diffidence and defensiveness both among school people and in the community. Communication becomes lax: many a good program has been lost in the passivity of an uninvolved community when the time came for evaluation and school board decision—or when some community group raised an unexpected alarm. A major reason for the failure of many school programs—especially in urban schools—is that school decisions have been made without reference to the views of the communities served. Students cannot be separated from their communities, and without community sanction implementation of major decisions may become impossible. Moreover, factions arise all too easily in the vacuum of an apathetic situation. If factions do not destroy a school system, they can be devastating to healthy growth.

The differences in perspective between community and school on matters of deep common concern are too marked and too significant for school policy to be determined within the arbitrary boundary of school administration or even of operating school personnel. The school board, legally vested with policy-making responsibility, is elected by the community but does not necessarily understand or represent all its multiplicity of interests and views.

A myriad of efforts have been spent in attempting to introduce community involvement in school decision making, but as those experienced with programs in inner-city schools have pointed out, it is very easy to present the task as impossible. Yet the alternative for school boards is to face increasing opposition to school expenditure, obstacles to innovative change, unexpected and sometimes militant attack, and increasing demands for "accountability" in the shape of quantitative evidence of pupil achievement. For the community, exclusion means a frustrating uncertainty of the directions which their schools are taking educationally, standing on the outside of a large share of their children's lives, voting expenditures without adequate information, and occasionally seeing school boards become a tight political sanctuary presiding over a demoralized school system.

As school districts are reorganized in larger units, whether for educational or economic reasons, the habit of excluding parents and other citizens decreases school involvement still further, and with it parental support of both student and school. Inability to follow school spending and budget preparation in independent consolidated districts opens doors to more generalized political attack. Larger numbers of students, separated from stabilizing community influences, are increasingly hard to organize in responsible operation. Thus the more that schools have sought to operate independently, the more they have increased their discipline problems and decreased their educational effectiveness.

RECENT PATTERNS OF COMMUNITY INVOLVEMENT
Whether school-community relationships were ever as easygoing as is sometimes attributed to prewar days may be questioned, but there was a time when a state commissioner of education could admonish a board of education that community help would have saved it a teachers' strike. The president of the Connecticut Parent-Teacher Association described the incident for National PTA:

> There have been extremely bad intracommunity relations, such as between teachers and the local board of education in Nor-

walk, Connecticut, . . . the so-called Norwalk strike. . . . In this instance [Alonzo G. Grace, then state commissioner of education] told both the teachers and the members of the board of education that had there been a balanced, functioning Council of Parent-Teacher Associations working in the community with the full support and cooperation of the local educators, such a situation could not have arisen. In Ansonia, Connecticut, another large industrial town, relations between the members of the board of education and the local educators grew so bad that the board refused to pay the teachers' salaries. Dr. Grace told the local citizens that had they good, balanced parent-teacher units that situation could not have developed.[2]

As word of these statements spread, school administrators in some numbers began to inquire into PTA membership; the PTA leadership responded by emphasizing the requirement of "balanced" membership (both parents and teachers) to all applicants. At that period not only were PTAs the most prevalent school-community organization, but school innovation and reform commonly came about through PTA action. The relationships were so close that the PTA had been able to work satisfactorily on a policy of "no interference with school administration" for nearly half a century. When discussions about educational policy are open and community views are taken into account in policy determination, there is little temptation to intervene at administrative levels.

During the rising tide of interest in education in the 1950s parents and many nonparent citizens flocked into the PTAs. At the height of its membership curve in 1963 National PTA's more than twelve million memberships nationwide[3] corresponded to a fair proportion of the forty million students in public schools.[4] Yet, even at this apparent high point in school-community cooperation, a fundamental change had occurred.

[2]Harry Overstreet and Bonaro Overstreet, *Where Children Come First*, National Congress of Parents and Teachers, [National PTA], Chicago, 1949, p. 121.

[3]*Proceedings*, National Congress of Parents and Teachers, Chicago, 1964, p. 230.

[4]*Statistical Abstract of the United States*, U.S. Department of Commerce, 1964, p. 121.

The Overstreets had written in 1949 that anyone moving into a new community might expect to find a PTA as he expected to find cars on the street, and they had observed that if there were not a PTA it would have to be invented. This was prophetic. With the postwar tide of professionalism, PTAs came to be seen as part of the school paraphernalia to be organized and controlled. As the constraints placed by school administrators upon PTA activities increased, the nature of PTAs began to change. Apathy spread widely. In 1965 a concerned National PTA undertook a three-year national self-study. Details of PTA activities were obtained from group interviews with local PTAs across the country selected as an accurate sample of the total membership. The professional publication *TRENDS in School Public Relations* offered its own perspective on one of the study reports:

> One of the shabbiest testimonials to the poor PR of American school administrators appears to be contained in the summaries of opinion interviews which have been conducted over the country by the National PTA Congress and are now being studied.
>
> PTA members, the unit group interviews indicate, are extremely unhappy about the way they are being treated by the schools. Instead of being aided to develop the kind of organizational and communication skills required to become a relevant force in improving parent education, home-school relations, and curriculum improvement, they have been sandbagged by school administrators into tasks for providing money and manpower.
>
> "The majority of school administrators do not invite PTA help," . . . the special committee studying the PTA organization . . . reported on the interviews in the October issue of the *National PTA Bulletin*. "The interpretation of PTA school cooperation policy has often been so strict as to discourage initiative for school improvement. When help in school improvement has not been invited, members have often lacked the skills to initiate improvement through the parent-teacher partnership. . . .
>
> "One-half of the PTAs said that the parent-teacher partnership and parent-teacher communication are in trouble," [the committee] reported. Less than one fourth of the PTA groups

reported having any current school or community improvement activity. "Instead, the great majority are providing equipment, manpower, or money for school support. . . . On the other hand, the large majority of these PTAs wanted change and wanted to do something about it."[5]

The findings were uncomfortable, and the hierarchic character of National PTA governance made difficult the needed changes to bring about a more flexible and member-oriented structure. One recommendation of the study committee was realized immediately: active support of student membership. Moreover, five members between the ages of fifteen and twenty were immediately added to the National PTA Board of Managers. Most have served two 2-year terms and all have been active and responsible members. As to other recommendations, persistent effort by succeeding groups of state PTA presidents have developed more collaborative mechanisms and member-responsiveness in the national governing group.

In the meantime member action brought about change in the basic school-PTA relationship. The millions of PTA members included very many who either shared the widespread discontent with schools or felt the pressures of rising dissatisfaction. Some Chicago PTAs, for instance, had to cope on the one hand with administrators who forbade PTA discussion of school problems on pain of being forbidden to hold their meetings in schools, and on the other hand with angry parents who insisted that PTA either represent their interests or give way to other vehicles. One resourceful leader trained parents in her home in the kind of educators' language which persuaded teachers to listen to their concerns. By such means the PTA remained a strong influence in the Chicago schools.

The Chicago members were among those who pressed for a change in the national bylaw which covered cooperation with schools. The desired change was finally adopted by the national convention in 1972, and national policy now formally stresses sharing in educational decision making rather than avoiding interference

[5]*TRENDS in School Public Relations*, National School Public Relations Association, Washington, D.C., Dec. 15, 1968, p. 2.

with administration. There is actually little difference in respect to the active collaboration which was always intended, but the new wording is no longer a screen for the timid or the cowardly.[6]

PTA is still the largest independent volunteer group in the country. Many school administrators, boards, and teachers value its partnership. In its tradition of concern for the whole world of children, PTAs still work in parent education, for health and social services, with juvenile courts, for safe environments, and human ecology. In many communities PTAs still struggle with the subtle demands of school control and with the handicaps of a hierarchic structure; but the character of the organization is changing toward a stronger school-community partnership as an increasing number of its leaders have learned the virtues and skills of involving members in joint decision making. It is still the only organization which involves the entire community and thus meets the criteria—open membership, open agenda, multiple leadership—of the open partnership.

Decentralization

In the meantime, the idea of a PTA in every town was being reinvented. Some groups confined themselves to a narrow concept of a fund-raising auxiliary which did not raise curriculum or policy questions. In other districts, frustrated parents organized "committees for quality education" and the like. Parents of youngsters with special problems reacted to school rejection of their concerns by building powerful lobbies for special education. Inner-city ghetto dwellers were particularly incensed with schools managed from "downtown" offices some miles away which gave poor attention to the needs of their children. These parents were frequently divided over whether they would work with or against schools. In many neighborhoods "cooperation" became an unusable term: "It only means doing what the schools want you to do," said a Boston parent.

---

[6]*National PTA Bylaws*, Article III, d. "The organization shall work with the schools to provide quality education for all children and youth and shall seek to participate in the decision-making process establishing school policy, recognizing that the legal responsibility has been delegated by the people to boards of education."

Inner-city leaders began to seek "community control" of their schools in the sense in which they conceived that citizens of suburban communities controlled their schools: that is, by local election of school boards. Thus a second definable movement in school-community relations appeared in New York, Philadelphia, Detroit, and elsewhere when central boards responded to community unrest with "decentralization" of school governance under locally elected district boards of education.

Because the district boards were locally elected, they were more accessible to their communities, but their actual powers were well short of their commitments. Decentralization did not confer "community control" of schools, but rather a variant of hierarchic governance. Particularly in New York, which has been the prototype of decentralization, the central board retained powers of contract negotiation and determination of faculty qualifications. Since the union negotiated with the central board for the entire city, the local boards met strong union opposition as they sought to employ their own choice of personnel, and were in turn accused of ethnic patronage in hiring. That is, local boards such as that of Ocean Hill–Brownsville wished to hire black faculty to teach black children, based on the conviction that a sense of black community was essential for strength in a pluralistic society: "Most blacks in this country want to stay here and want to participate in the social order as equals with full preservation of their ethnic differences. Thus black power is a means to an end—inclusion."[7]

Barbara Sizemore described both Ocean Hill–Brownsville in New York and the Woodlawn Experimental Schools Project in Chicago as based on the strategy of group solidarity to win power away from the establishment for the redistribution of resources.[8] She blamed what she described as the failure of both experiments on lack of power. Her account indicated, however, that in addition to lacking

---

[7]Barbara A. Sizemore, "Community Power and Education." *Education for an Open Society*, Association for Supervision and Curriculum Development, Washington, D.C., 1974, p. 134.

[8]Ibid., p. 113.

certain powers the boards turned to exclusionary tactics instead of uniting their communities, and that these tactics proved to be self-defeating.

> Like Ocean Hill–Brownsville, the project [Woodlawn] was designed for failure because of the following limitations: (*a*) authority was not clearly defined; (*b*) the entire constituency was not represented by TWO (The Woodlawn Organization); (*c*) the power of the WCB (Woodlawn Community Board) derived from preexisting bases which preserved institutional loyalties; (*d*) the WCB lacked approval-veto powers; and (*e*) the WCB had no control over money. TWO collaborated with the administration and supported unilateral decision making excluding students and teachers, thereby contradicting the goals of the project. This support affirmed the existing bureaucratic order and all the other external offices higher than the school. The community organization, allegedly fighting for local control, actually supported more bureaucratic and less aggregate grass-roots decision making. In the end it lost the chance to evaluate teachers. No other project had had that opportunity. . . . With no union to fight, TWO had to create the issue of teacher opposition. Consequently it failed to recognize the fruits of power when the teachers extended them. . . . In the end, it was pushed into the untenable position of advocating police action against its own youth. TWO had become part of the problem.[9]

The goals of identity and inclusion are necessary to all groups, but the tactic of exclusion of concerned groups or individuals by intent or by negligence has negative and sometimes disastrous consequences. The goal of inclusion is incompatible with the pursuit of power by and for one group, whatever the injustices which may give rise to the effort. Those who adopt adversary methods as major strategy tend to defeat themselves, whether by mistaking their real interests in the fascination of a more glittering objective, by tiring their allies, or by leading others to combine against them.

Decentralization in New York seems to have had relatively little influence of itself on the effectiveness of schools. A study by Melvin

[9]Ibid., pp. 133–134.

Zimet[10] offers little evidence of change in reading scores, student absenteeism or suspension, vandalism, faculty absenteeism, or faculty transfers. The study suggests that the decentralized boards put more responsibility on schools for student learning than had existed previously, and the community had somewhat more influence in the schools. It also suggests that the limitations on their powers and the divisiveness of the prescribed election process forced the local boards into following the same pattern of closed decision making and isolation from the community as central boards tend to do.

Perhaps another report about New York schools offered a better key to factors in school effectiveness. The New York State Office of Education Performance published a study of two elementary schools with similar characteristics and differing effectiveness. Both schools were largely black and Hispanic in enrollment, with more than 90 percent of the students eligible for free lunches, and had heavily white staffs. In one school more than half the pupils were reading at or above grade level on state standards, while in the other school only 10 percent met the same standards.

> In the more successful school there was "a collaborative relationship between parents, pupils and staff," the report noted. The other school was "characterized by divisiveness, disorder, and disillusionment" and the school's staff generally attributed children's reading problems to factors beyond their control."[11]

Community Schools

A very different movement has focused on providing ghetto children with effective education through direct and intensive involvement of parents in operation of "community schools." In Washington the Morgan School community negotiated an arrangement with the city school board delegating certain powers to the community, although

---

[10]Melvin Zimet, *Decentralization and School Effectiveness*, Teachers College Press, New York, 1973.
[11]*The New York Times*, Apr. 4, 1974. © 1974 by The New York Times Company. Reprinted by permission.

the school had a contract with Antioch College in Ohio, which actually managed the school. In Boston a series of community schools were organized and governed by parents and supported by their own fund-raising efforts, sometimes with the help of foundations or universities interested in educational experiments. These schools initiated the use of a parent in the classroom as equal partner with a certified teacher. As Doreen Wilkinson pointed out, the middle-class white teachers, upon whom the schools were initially dependent, were well-intentioned but unable to deal knowledgeably with the children. The parent, on the other hand "was an actual neighbor of many of the children, someone whom the children could respect, whose authority they would accept. . . . A well-chosen person from the community, working in a spirit of genuine cooperation with the teacher, can provide the necessary ingredient of reality, thus creating a classroom environment conducive to learning, and at the same time giving the children a living example of racial and social equality."[12]

The handful of community schools struggled under fiscal handicaps. They had some foundation help, although this tended to carry educational conditions which added to difficulties of governance; at the same time the schools had to be kept small in order to keep the close community involvement which was the basis of their educational philosophy. Some of their educational patterns, however, such as the partnership roles of parents, influenced and were carried over to other schools.

The use of the term "community school" by these parent-run schools should not be confused with the different and far broader community school movement initiated by Frank J. Manly and Charles Stewart Mott in Flint, Michigan, in the 1930s, later supported by the Mott Foundation, and consolidated as the National Community School Education Association in 1966. Community

---

[12]Doreen H. Wilkinson, *Community Schools: Education for Change*, National Association of Independent Schools, Boston, November 1973, pp. 14–55. Written from a background of involvement with the education of black children during most of its recent phases, this small book is valuable for access to several minority perspectives.

schools in this concept number several thousand across the country. They seek to serve the entire community, all age groups, all interests. Their intent is to make the existing school plant a community center by encouraging community groups to use the buildings and providing a number of public and voluntary services, including health and social services as well as education.

These community schools have brought about little if any change in school governance, and it is doubtful whether there was any such intent in the concept. PTAs and other community groups have joined many educators in promoting the concept of community schools as a means of involving more people in the schools, increasing available community centers, and combating problems of alienation, dropouts, and vandalism. In accomplishing these ends, community schools have served as catalytic agents in developing leadership to mobilize community resources and thus have brought about a degree of community involvement in governance decisions.

School Volunteers

Still another strong trend in community involvement is the recruiting of specific parent or other citizen help as school volunteers or in advisory committees. Neither volunteers nor advisory committees began from school initiatives. As late as 1960 most teachers rejected the idea of sharing the classroom with other adults. By the end of that decade, however, volunteers were actively recruited and are now a common feature of many classrooms.

The change came about partly because parents wanted to be involved with their children in school and to understand this environment, partly because of the devoted efforts of concerned citizens who saw that schools needed help, and to some degree because of the increase in student teaching, which provided a model. It may now be hard to recall the great care with which lay volunteers were introduced into the schools, and the cautious steps that were taken to allay any feelings of threat and interference among the teachers. One of the early programs was School Volunteers for Boston, initiated in 1965. This group developed a three-to-four-week training program for its volunteers before they entered the schools and continuously monitors the progress of volunteers with the school principals.

For several years volunteers were not allowed to work where their own children were in school. Later on, both the unrest in urban schools and the growing school population made the teachers more willing to accept another adult in the classroom and less restrictive in their requirements. The growth of open education and the premium that it places on adult-child interaction increased the number of both paraprofessionals and parent volunteers. With more than two million volunteers in schools across the country, the movement was recognized at the federal level for a time by the establishment of a program in the Office of Education called Volunteers in Education. A professional organization called the National School Volunteer Program was established in the late 1960s to share information and assistance among program directors.

In schools where volunteer aides are accepted, teachers have learned to value them. While the greater part of volunteer time is probably taken up with clerical chores, the volunteers' interaction with children becomes a useful teaching aid. Volunteers provide a bridge to the community, a sense of community support in the classroom, and an everyday perspective on community thinking for the teacher. While volunteers work specifically under the teacher's direction, there is a partnership and a subtle decision sharing about children which has benefited many a youngster.

Advisory Committees

The growth of advisory committees began with the discovery by interested citizens that ad hoc committees were an effective way to bring about change in schools through fact-finding and persuasion. Citizen movements brought about the first regional school districts in New England, for instance, soon after World War II. It was not long before school administrators found committee help useful in all sorts of problems, especially after the administrative habit of intervening for "safe" PTA presidents eroded PTA's once solid support base. Advisory committees helped to convince taxpayers of the utility of new programs and the soundness of school budgets. A survey by the editors of *Education U.S.A.* found that the tasks assigned to advisory committees now cover almost every area of school program, organization, and policy: philosophy, finance, public relations, construction, personnel, transportation, desegregation, and student discipline. In some instances the advisers even act as ombudsmen and grievance committees. Survey returns led to an estimate that less than 5 percent of all school districts are without advisory committees of one sort or another.[13]

The administrative view of advisory committee powers was, in general, that they were advisory only. One respondent wrote, "Some individuals find it hard to accept the fact that their work and recommendations will not necessarily be totally accepted."[14] Although it may seem unfair to allow a group to work hard and produce recommendations in ignorance of board interests and inclinations, this is a common occurrence. If there were appropriate interchange between board and advisory committee, members of the advisory committee would be able to deal realistically with differences.

One of the exceptions to the general view reported in the survey was a district in Brooklyn, New York, whose respondent stated that while the committee's authority was "technically advisory," it was "de facto unlimited"; the school board had not rejected a single recommendation in five years.[15] Some school authorities cited advantages in "two-way communication," "parent involvement," and "democratized administration," in addition to getting needed jobs done at small expense to the taxpayer. Some suggested warnings about using a committee as a "rubber stamp," a "shock absorber," a "promoter," or a "bailer out." The editors concluded that if a school system were in trouble for poor policies or administration, a citizen group used in such a way would not long ward off trouble and would even increase distrust eventually. They urged that a school

---

[13]*Citizens Advisory Committees: Current Trends in School Policies and Programs*, National School Public Relations Association, Arlington, Va., 1973, p. 7.
[14]Ibid., p. 26.
[15]Ibid., p. 9.

system would be well advised to support the credibility of its advisory committee by respecting its independence.

It would appear that the degree to which advisory committees shared in decision making was partly determined by the kind of tasks they were assigned, whether public relations or similar "chores," or broader tasks such as long-range planning in which the kind of thinking developed can be more influential. In general, the good relations between board and advisory committee reported by most of NSPRA's respondents suggest that most citizens are pleased with involvement and influence as a means of decision sharing, when this is allowed to occur. The evidence indicated that with this sort of relationship advisory committees could make their best contribution in working on goals, long-range planning, major curriculum revision, and organizational change.

THE ADVOCATES OF ADVERSARY ACTION

Despite these available devices and practices, actual decision sharing is still very much on the fringes of school governance. Volunteers and advisory committee members are more often appointed on some sort of compatibility test than openly recruited. School systems are wary of "too much" community involvement. As one principal told his PTA, having parents in school is like using salt in baking bread: enough is enough.

Thus it is somewhat baffling to find it axiomatic in professional literature that citizens must be encouraged to find a role in public education. The *Education U.S.A.* editors of the advisory committee survey put it urgently: "The administrator and board that make no effort to involve citizens, or involve them only in a window-dressing role, sooner or later pay the piper either in steady loss of support or a cataclysmic outbreak."[16] We have seen all of these results: decided loss of support, bond issues and school levies voted down, superintendents dismissed, school boards turned out at election, and violent protest. All of these occur often enough to keep school boards and

[16]Ibid., p. 28.

administrators in some uneasiness—not so often, however, as to bring about much change in their views of appropriate governance. Citizens still have very little to say about their schools.

In such a climate of frustration, there has spread a wide acceptance of conflict as a necessary model of participation in school policy decision making. Several prominent groups have put forward proposals for vesting counterbalancing powers in citizen councils, what Don Davies has called a "third force" in education.[17] In Massachusetts the Governor's Commission on Citizen Participation reported in December 1973 recommendations for citizens' councils with "powers sufficient to insure that they cannot be ignored or manipulated by a truculent bureaucracy." Such powers would include broad policy formulation, determination of budget priorities, "serving as an ombudsman for citizen-consumer complaints, and acting as an appeals forum to resolve clashes of interest in program goals and procedures."[18]

A second recommendation for citizen councils with substantial powers came from the National Committee for Citizens in Education (NCCE). Between June and October 1974 NCCE invited concerned citizens to speak to problems of school governance in "hearings" held in five major cities across the country: Minneapolis, St. Louis, Portland, Atlanta, and Los Angeles. The record developed a long list of complaints about poor education and poor treatment, many of which were vigorously denied by school authorities. The net of the evidence argues a poor state of communication between the anxious respondents and the responsible school people. A professional observer who attended all five hearings wrote of the change which the testimony brought about in his own views:

> If someone would have asked me last year if citizens and parents have a role in public education, I would have answered that they do control the schools through the election of state and

[17]Don Davies, "The Emerging Third Force in Education," *Inequality in Education*, Harvard University, Center for Law and Education, Cambridge, Mass., November 1973.

[18]*Report of the Governor's Commission on Citizen Participation*, Commonwealth of Massachusetts, Boston, December 1973.

local school boards and through the many parent advisory groups surrounding each building and district. The testimony at the NCCE hearings repeatedly bombarded me with examples of parent involvement programs. Just as I was about to internally nod with satisfaction, another parent group would tell us in convincing tones that the program wasn't working. At the first and second hearings I found myself, "yes, buting" what I had heard. Yes, but if they would have introduced a plan in more organized fashion, if they would have had more parent involvement, if they would have had different people involved, etc. In short, the six days of hearings used up all of my "yes, but" excuses and eventually brought me to the conclusion that parent/citizen involvement programs just don't come off as an honest attempt to involve parents in what happens to their children in school. Parents, in my opinion, want to see their children's education attainment progress each year, not just when they are lucky enough to get a caring teacher or when they are placed in a building with a good principal or when a whole host of other variables (usually not controlled by the parent) are all met. The frustration of seeing a simple goal, such as reading, be continually pushed just out of the parents' reach while precious time passes and children's attitudes gradually harden towards school, brings out a level of concern in parents equal to someone causing them physical harm. Seeing the education needs of a child as a parent sees them is not an easy task for professional educators. The gap between how well most educators think they accomplish this feat and how well parents think they accomplish it is much wider than I ever thought. It was the constant awareness that this gap existed and the consistent offering of testimony, some in unsophisticated terms, that eventually led me to my second assumption—that the education profession is too overprofessionalized.[19]

The problem Chris Pipho described so well touches many parents in most schools, and basically because most professional people are content with one-way communication. It occurs literally to very few teachers, administrators, or board members that they can learn anything by listening to parents. Most students of this impasse

---

[19]Christian C. Pipho, "Comments on the Educational Governance Hearings Conducted by the National Committee for Citizens in Education," n.p., n.d.

agree that two-way communication is the first and basic necessity, but there are wide differences as to both means and objectives.

It was Dr. Pipho's recommendation that legislation be enacted to ensure that parents be allowed time off from jobs to visit schools and consult with teachers on the educational progress of their children, in the same manner as released time is mandated for voting or jury duty.

NCCE's own recommendations centered on an elected council at each school to "share authority and responsibility for curriculum, school program, budgeting, school progress reports, and personnel evaluations." One of its important functions would be participation in selection of the principal. Its basic function would be to balance the interests of the professional people and those whom they serve.[20]

A third recommendation of this sort came from a National Task Force for High School Reform established by the Charles F. Kettering Foundation. The report of this group described a "third force" in education as "the consciousness of the community . . . that public control means what it says, . . . driven by the sense that the high school is evolving into a self-perpetuating bureaucratic institution" and that "as an institution it has become its own first priority.[21] As a movement for reform, said the Task Force, citizen involvement "must itself be institutionalized."[22] The report offered a series of recommendations which included these: that all legal barriers to total community involvement in the schools be removed;[23] that a widely representative group be formed in each community, with opportunities to increase skills in communication, problem solving, and decision making with assistance from outside the schools;[24] that

[20]*Public Testimony on Public Schools*, National Committee for Citizens in Education, McCutchan Publishing Corporation, Berkeley, Calif., 1975, pp. 221–222. Copyright © 1975 by McCutchan Publishing Corporation. Reprinted by permission of the publisher.

[21]*The Adolescent, Other Citizens, and Their High Schools: A Report to the Public and the Profession,* the Report of Task Force '74, McGraw-Hill, New York, 1975, p. 9.

[22]Ibid., p. 10.

[23]Ibid., p. 10.

[24]Ibid., p. 109.

day-to-day decisions of operating the schools should remain with school administrators and teachers,[25] but that community school boards be established for individual schools for participation, with veto powers, in the selection of principals, evaluation of teachers, authorization of instructional programs, and approval of local building plans, within centrally approved budgets. The district school board would be limited to general policy formation, budget preparation, and review.[26]

Still another recommendation for elected building councils has come from a Massachusetts study by the Institute for Responsive Education under Dr. Davies' direction. This group recommended legislation to authorize elected school-community councils for individual school sites; the recommendation differed from the others that have been cited in that the members would include students, teachers, and other citizens as well as parents, but at least 51 percent of the members would be parents of children in the school. Its duties would include participation with the principal in assessing educational needs of the community, development and evaluation of programs and curricula, definition of educational goals, long-range planning, budget review and recommendations for budget priorities, screening and recommending candidates for principal, development and implementation of personnel evaluation processes, improving school-community relations, and assessment of school performance. "Cooperation" would be "required" of school committees, including sharing of all legally public information.[27]

School Building Councils and Community Interests

All four recommendations assume that elected school building councils would improve community participation in school decision making. All four came from groups whose members or leaders are or have been practicing educators, generally administrators. The stated

[25]Ibid., p. 11.
[26]Ibid., p. 110.
[27]Institute for Responsive Education, *Together: Schools and Communities*, Massachusetts Advisory Council on Education, Boston, August 1975, pp. 99–103.

intent in each case is to redress imbalance of power between school and community, and to make a reality of the right of the community to participate in educational decision making.

There appears to be no constitutional obstacle to the proposed shift of governance powers. State legislatures have established school boards and could modify or divide their powers. Their feasibility is another matter.

The dynamics of such a scheme would place a school building council either in the hierarchic pattern, subject to school board direction as are the decentralized district boards in New York City, or in an independent and competitive position. Two of the four recommendations took the latter alternative, with a separation between "general" and "building" policies. It is not clear how board and council could effectively distinguish between general policies and building policies, even with the best of intentions. For instance, the determination of faculty qualifications and evaluation procedures were specified for building council determination and yet are regularly a matter of interest in teacher negotiations between the school board and the district bargaining agent. Such were the issues between the Ocean Hill–Brownsville district board and the United Federation of Teachers (UFT) which led to strikes and court action in 1968.

Again, a time of scarce funds places the ranking of such interests as special education, cultural arts, and "basic studies" at high priority for both board and building council. If there were money for only one or some very limited number of additional teachers (or program), whose priority would be honored—that of the district board or that of the building council, of the existing faculty, the principal, or the parents?

With the elected building councils essentially competitive to school boards, especially if they were endowed with veto powers, policy differences would almost inevitably put the school building administration in an unenviable middle position. The councils might well develop curricular and extracurricular proposals contrary to established budget restrictions or to negotiated contracts which had become board policy. If the councils invoked their powers as recommended, administrators and faculty might be forced into a position where questions of survival superseded questions of educating boys and girls.

The original objective for citizen councils was "community control," or a balance of power. But if "sides" develop, and both sides have equal power, and if neither gives in or is willing to negotiate, actually neither has power. The outcome is stalemate, in which programs are not moved forward and problems are not moved toward solution. This has been illustrated not only in some New York City districts, but in the history of some Title I parent advisory committees or PACs (mandated by the Elementary and Secondary Education Act) in states such as Massachusetts where the committees were given veto power over Title I plans. Because the urban community had learned such deep distrust of school boards in some cities, and Title I committees were not given preparation in collaborative skills, adversary positions and sometimes stalemates developed. School authorities have found the stalemates irritating, but in a political encounter the PACs have seldom won. Leaders whom school authorities found aggressive have been isolated from their constituencies, somewhat in the same manner as PACs have been used to displace open-membership PTAs: "The PACs can get things from the school which we cannot," has been a common complaint.

The four recommendations to transfer powers from school boards to building councils were further based on the ground that councils would be more representative of the community. The question arises, however, whether councils of any fixed membership could be much more representative than school boards. They are not a substitute for general citizen involvement; moreover, they would tend to prevent other citizen involvement. The elected council would tend to become the recognized channel of reference for all community concerns. It could easily monopolize the principal's attention, although its members might not be representative of community concerns, and thereby discourage general school-community communication. Moreover, if such a council were elected as representative of community groups, its members could well tend to be competitive for constituent interests, rather than collaborative for a general purpose. Another disturbing factor is the habitually small vote which has elected New York district boards, with its frequently factional character, and the small vote which elected biracial building councils in Boston under the federal court's desegregation order; both suggest an increase in citizen apathy. If the community is further separated from its school rather than drawn closer by the institution of the school council, the council would tend to become isolated from its constituency, as New York's district boards are observed to have done, and therefore lose their community base.

The building council proposal has a tempting organizational neatness about it, a solution applied from outside and above; with a long-handled spoon, so to speak, the legislature or state educational agency could solve local school-community problems. The proposal does not recognize that if people are truly desirous of participation in solving their own problems, they ordinarily prefer to involve themselves. The structural pattern may evolve less tidily, but with adequate opportunity and information the solutions which concerned groups work out for themselves are more pertinent and more lasting. One of the most active self-described "change agents" of the 1960s suggested in 1971 that he had learned this "the hard way."

> I had a certain concept of reform—say like team teaching or educational technology, and I would go into a school system and try and manipulate the situation so it would come out my way. Now I feel this is a wrong strategy to use. We must stop pushing people around even though it is done inadvertently, even though it is being done in the name of reform. It never worked in the past, and I fear it will never work in the future, because the strategy was wrong.[28]

Placing people in inappropriately competitive and adversary positions is a species of "pushing people around." Political solutions for educational problems, such as the election of representative

[28]Mario Fantini, from a speech delivered at the Wingspread Conference of the National Consortium on Educational Alternatives, Nov. 8, 1971, *Changing Schools*, No. 002, Educational Alternatives Project, Indiana University, Bloomington, n.d.

school boards, are more appropriate to district and state levels than to the local school itself. Here the quality of education is directly related to the quality of interaction between teacher and student, and, second only to this, to the quality of relationships between principal and faculty, and between principal, faculty, and parents. The intervention of political action at this point is an obstacle to its own objective. A citizen council at school level is an exclusionary device, unlikely either to foster collaborative relationships or to achieve the desired citizen influence in school operation.

The more practical alternative is to encourage all interested individuals, lay and professional, to come together on any matter of common interest, in developmental discussions, where they can learn to understand each other and influence each other's thinking. Participation in assessing educational needs, setting goals, development and evaluation of programs, long-range planning, and budget priority review are all feasible activities, provided that the group includes all who are concerned and builds from one objective to another in valid collaboration.

Out of such collective action comes real power, if power is significant, to influence curriculum and school practices. But it is not institutionalized power. Collaboration is a process, not any particular organization or any particularly assigned powers or set of accommodations. Provision for ad hoc groups, with open membership and open agenda, recognizes the reality that parents, teachers, students, and other citizens are interested in pursuing different problems at different times, and could be prevented from taking any action by the protocol of channeling discussions through an elected school council. Therefore it should be made possible for the process to be initiated by any interested individuals who raise a concern of sufficient interest to attract others to a discussion. In doing so they might or might not utilize existing voluntary, open-membership groups.

The partnership schools described in the second chapter offer examples both of the process through which ad hoc groups may develop educational ideas, such as Manchester High School's expanded curriculum program, and of partnership governance through an open-member organization such as Barbour Elementary School's PTA. An instance of another sort came from a respondent to the *Education U.S.A.* survey of advisory councils. At the time of the survey Los Angeles had had three years' experience with such building-level advisory committees or councils. Evaluation at the end of the first year brought about in-service training for council members and provision for "more realistic participation." The councils were enlarged to include school staff, students, and other community members as well as parents. Subsequently the principal of one school reported:

> While our council was initially concerned with how Title I money was spent at our school, it has since widened its scope considerably and has become highly influential in furthering progress at Cortez. With the aid and support of our council, Cortez has launched a number of projects to encourage cooperation and participation.[29]

These examples illustrate an essential characteristic for successful collaboration, and one significant difference among the four proposals for elected school councils. Three proposals increased the adversary character of their recommendations by placing only nonprofessional citizens in their elected councils; the fourth included teachers, students, and administrators, as well as parents and other nonprofessional citizens. Mixed membership helps to avoid the dichotomy of interests and the strained relationships which are often a problem of citizen advisory committees in making suggestions for school faculties. Even more important, it helps to ameliorate the adversary relationships so prevalent between professional and nonprofessional citizens concerned with schools.

On this ground one may question a further recommendation for separate and militant parents' groups in the report of the Kettering Foundation's Task Force '74. Exclusively parent groups are common among public and private schools, but almost always as either a fund-raising auxiliary or as a means of communication to parents.

---

[29]*Citizens Advisory Committees*, p. 29.

The outstanding example of a parent advocacy group is probably the United Parents Association in New York City, "a power group which will fight for the schools when they think it in the interest of their children but, equally important, will fight the schools when they deem it necessary."[30] A strong factor in the militancy of the United Parents was the growing strength of the teachers' union and the adversary stance toward parents taken by union leadership. "Parents are no allies of teachers," wrote Albert Shanker, UFT president. "In any strike parents think more of their own inconvenience than of the merits of the teachers' cause."[31]

This is the adversary model which Task Force '74 specifically recommended "as a national model." Repeating the advice often given National PTA by labor leaders who object to teacher membership in PTA, the report continued: "What is most needed is to take the 'T' out of PTA . . . the PTA should become an association of *parents taking action*."[32]

Such a development would complete the adversary framework—a fantasy which if realized would model a new militancy among youth and make humane education almost impossible. Fortunately, the independent and collaborative instincts of very many people who care about youngsters take a different course. As we have seen, much collaboration is taking place among all who are concerned with schools.

Nevertheless, the advocacy of the conflict model does often succeed in stifling an emergent collaboration. In the light of the New York experience, one can doubt whether union advice for separate parent and teacher organization is other than self-serving. One can doubt, also, whether a significant increase in "parent power" could avoid leading to narrower interests and a chilling of parent-teacher relationships.

[30]Dan W. Dodson, "Authority, Power, and Education," *Education for an Open Society*, Association for Supervision and Curriculum Development, Washington, D.C., 1974, p. 102.

[31]Albert Shanker, "Teacher Unionism: A Quiet Revolution . . . ," *The New York Times*, Oct. 28, 1973.

[32]*The Adolescent, Other Citizens, and Their High Schools*, op. cit., p. 30.

COMMUNITY INITIATIVES FOR PARTNERSHIP

Community people usually have to find their own legitimacy for participation in school affairs. If there were no other evidence of the walls which have grown up between school and community it would appear in the almost universal question among parents and other laymen who want involvement: "Where can we start?"

To develop a partnership from community initiative in the present climate of schools, one builds with steps of inquiry and involvement. Probably the first step is self-assurance that involvement with schools is essential and in the best interests of children, and a resolution not to be discouraged. The quick dismay in a teacher's face at the request to visit classes out of season (that is, outside American Education Week), the school board meeting room with no empty chairs, the public relations letter from school which obviously expects no reply: all of these are common. They are disturbing to parents and other citizens, but they are more likely to arise from ignorance, defensiveness, and previous lack of communication than from ill will. There is a strong temptation to respond with resentment. As we have seen, many groups and individuals have responded in terms of power initiatives, measures which tend to harden rather than soften prickly relationships. On the other hand, if parents and other citizens use friendly and collaborative methods of involving themselves, and use them effectively, one may be substantially certain that the school people who rejected the initial overture will share pride and pleasure in a successful partnership outcome.

In working with teachers, for instance, a parent will find that some teachers are simply timid of parents and in all likelihood have never had professional preparation for dealing with laymen. Some may be limited by a definite school board policy which restricts visits and communication. In either case, however, the parent can achieve fellowship with the teacher by taking the approach of sharing the teacher's concern for the student. If the parent can find a tactful way of involving the student in a parent-teacher conference, the conversation is likely to be more honest and considerate, and therefore more positive and constructive. Without the student present, parent and teacher are frequently talking about two different people.

Sometimes it is hard for parents and teachers to move out of their respective roles and talk with each other as "people," but with effort parents can usually find some common interests for beginning a friendly relationship. PTA programs are intended to foster the development of pleasant acquaintance. Out of these conversations, at some point, the teacher may be persuaded that a parent's observation of the child in class may be useful to their joint understanding of the child's needs. Even to those teachers who are convinced that classrooms are a territorial prerogative not to be invaded, a gradual change in perspective comes with study groups, workshops, perhaps with periodic exchanges of ideas over coffee. In this process both teacher and parent find they are learning from each other.

As parents discover that school situations are more complicated than the parent-teacher relationship, they begin to ask, "Why does this happen, or why does that not happen?" As often as not, an apparently simple question requires an elaborate answer, which may or may not be known to any one teacher or administrator questioned. The parent may go from one to another authority, and find each one frustratingly unresponsive.

Some parents begin to attend school board meetings in search of answers. They may be treated cordially; the extra chairs appear, and board meeting proceedings may be gracefully interrupted to meet their concerns. On the other hand, they may be treated in such a manner as to receive a message that citizen attendance is unwanted and out of order. PTA members attending as organization representatives have sometimes felt so badly treated as to refuse to return. The usual reception is between these extremes.

In whatever case there are some simple procedures to learn for acceptable citizen participation in school board meetings. Most states have open-meeting laws applicable to school boards which allow closed or "executive" sessions only for a few specified topics. During periods other than these, the fact that there may be no extra chairs or that the room is small may not be used to prevent citizen attendance. If a citizen wishes to make a presentation, or ask a question, a letter to the chairman a week or ten days before the meeting should assure a place on the agenda and will place the matter of concern in the school board record. Ordinarily a limited amount of time is accorded citizen presentations, so that careful preparation will make the most of the allotted minutes. If the request for time is refused, the request may be repeated, or other steps taken. If the presentation is accepted, board members may ask some questions, but unless they choose to act at that moment, further discussion of the matter will take place later in the meeting and the citizen questioner may not expect to have a part in it.

Sometimes it takes hard listening and strategic questioning over a series of meetings to understand what a school board is about. Time is well spent, however, in gaining first-hand knowledge of the institutional fabric. In learning to know their board members as people, and as much as possible about the legal and fiscal limitations under which the board operates, citizens learn something of where their own influence is useful.

Upon occasion something unexpected appears. In one small town PTA leaders were concerned about school expenditures and discovered by accident that the school board had not been paying its bills over a substantial period. They requested information, and when this was denied, asked to see the fiscal records. After considerable discussion over the question of the public's right to inform itself of the public's business, the PTA leadership did prevail. It was discovered that the school board had misjudged the size of its obligation to the regional high school district serving its older students and concealed the problem until new revenues made up the difference. The situation was clarified, and the outcome was relief on the part of the school committee and subsequent reasonably good working relationships.

In a different sort of situation, a PTA council was of substantial assistance to a school board. Council leaders shared a general suspicion of collusion in the letting of school building contracts. School construction was controlled not by the school board but by a committee of city government. With the help of an architects' group and the city newspapers, the PTA council supported an inquiry and publication of findings, and then undertook a successful campaign to change the city charter to place responsibility for school construction with the school board.

While the examples of effective political action by PTAs may be better known to this writer, the requisite political skills are well distributed. Citizens use such skills with school boards to secure program changes with fair frequency, in fact rather more frequently than professional people like. It may be said that school programs should be responsive to the community. Even so, parents or other citizens who take specific proposals directly to the school board for enactment and implementation are bypassing essential elements in the decision-making process, elements which make decisions credible and eventually determine the quality of implementation.

It takes more than a school board vote to give legitimacy to a new program. It takes sufficient involvement of those concerned or affected in the actual development of a program to create willingness to share in its implementation. Otherwise the impetus for implementation which may be generated by a school board or administrative directive is gradually lost in the inertia of the institutional fabric. Or, the proposal may have bypassed essential interests and should not be implemented.

The long sequence of involvement which ends in useful program change might start with a layman's question as well as with an administrative pipe dream or a faculty discussion, and often does. Let us suppose that somebody's question, "Why does such and such happen, or why does it not happen?" has been raised and unsatisfactorily answered. How can a citizen secure serious professional attention? After raising the question once or twice, parents (and others) sometimes feel that insistence might raise some sort of confrontation. Parents do worry about reaction which might touch their own children, whether reasonably or not. One disarming alternative is for two or three to ask for assistance in understanding the matter.

"Can we talk with you?" is a request hard for any one to refuse.

"We are concerned about something we think important. Can we talk about it?" "There are some practices we should like to know more about. Can we meet with you?" "Can you help us discuss something we are concerned about?"

Such questions establish respect, honest concern, and a reasonable request for information. They are likely to avoid the rejoinder, "This is school business," or, "You will have to take this to the school board." If the welfare of one's own children or of the children of the school is involved, it is appropriate not to take "no" for an answer, in any case. The questions may be asked in other ways, by other people. If refusal may be anticipated, three or four or five people should go together—a sufficient number to establish a community concern, and not so large a number as to suggest a confrontation.

The ensuing discussion may lead to a sufficient clarification of the question at issue, and a useful base for other friendly interaction will have been established. If it is agreed, however, that further discussion is needed, the next step is to propose to open the discussion to all who may be interested? If objection is raised, such as, "Why would anyone else be interested?" a response could be, "Let's find out." Or, "I should prefer to keep this among ourselves," could be met with: "We know there are others who are interested, and we should prefer not to be in the position of trying to speak for them."

It is important to consider carefully who else might be interested and therefore specifically invited. Who should be interested is generally equivalent to who is affected. At the same time it is essential to publicize the opportunity in such a way as to reach everyone who might possibly be interested. The question of numbers may be raised as an objection, but numbers can always be dealt with satisfactorily through organization.

It is equally important to insist upon a continuing open membership. Even the apparently uninterested and apathetic have interests and concerns to be reckoned with; they may decide to become involved late in the day, or they may feel sufficiently protected by the fact of open membership and therefore lend quiet but useful support.

In general, however, as Elliot Richardson is said to have pointed out, people like to be in at the takeoff as well as the landing.

An alternative to raising one's questions with school authority is to sit down with one or two others to test one's questions and ideas for significance and clarity. If others are interested, the group should gradually be enlarged to include teachers as well as parents, and also administrators, school board members, and other citizens who may explore the questions at issue from different points of view. If a variety of people find the ideas interesting, the same open invitations should be offered.

A third alternative approach is the use of existing organizations. Either lay or professional people may ask for a PTA or PAC agenda item in order to raise a topic for general discussion, and to follow initial discussion with a proposal for an open study group of interested members. Use of an existing organization offers an available audience, and perhaps an immediate constituency of persons who are already working together; but it should be a compatible organization whose sponsorship would be desirable, should its members decide to offer it.

IS EVERYBODY HERE?

The purpose of drawing together all who are concerned with a problem is to build a program that meets all needs involved. This can only be accomplished if the many successive decisions that contribute to a total program are shared by those who will be involved in its implementation or affected by resulting change.

Thus it is important that community people who initiate change not neglect to involve school personnel in their discussions, and that they be watchful for the mix of lay and professional people in discussions of common interests. Groups tend to develop cohesiveness, and a like-minded group will tend to develop an unconscious exclusiveness. If interests of lay and professional people on a given question develop separately, adversary positions may develop which are likely to cause unnecessary difficulty. Mixed groups can work out questions as they arise.

Moreover, mixed groups stimulate each other to more analytical thinking and thus are usually more productive than like-minded groups. There is a magic in open discussion among people of different backgrounds who are seeking common objectives that creates colleagueship. Given only the basic assumption that schools are a shared concern, the negative feelings about role differences tend to disappear in the exploration of ideas and their implications for children. That is, members of the discussion tend to forget who is a parent and who is a teacher, or other role, in identifying people with their ideas and other contributions. The process leads to feelings of equality.

Unlike an elitist or other homogeneous group, the cohesiveness which such a group develops tends to be open to newcomers, because newcomers will be seen as sources of new ideas and new knowledge. Thus beginning with the question, "Who else should be here?" is crucially important.

For instance, many interest groups postpone involving members of the power structure, whether school board members or other "influentials behind the scenes," with the thought that they should "build strength" before announcing their proposals. Involving such people at the outset simply because they should be interested will avoid any appearance of threat and therefore a later impasse, or perhaps something more dangerous. It is a poor return to school people who have joined in a matter of community interest to involve them in some explosive and far-reaching controversy. The continuing possibility of such an untoward outcome is one reason why school people are frightened of community involvement. The only real insurance against this possibility is for group members to be continually interested in hearing and involving all who have related concerns. Most violent reactions arise from frustration at not being heard or involved; extra time and patience to this end are well invested.

It follows that issues should be raised as members find them pertinent, whether or not they may be controversial. It is understood that people come with different sets of values and different interests. They should share these early in their discussions. Thereafter each person carries two responsibilities, two roles, as it were: presentation of one's own views, and proposals with each other's interests in mind. The second question, then, is "Who are we? Why are we here?"

The third step is fact-finding. Accurate and adequate information is the necessary base for any productive discussion. A very simple organization of fact-finding subcommittees can develop necessary information for the group to use to arrive at pertinent decisions and eventual program recommendations.[33]

During the entire period, keeping the community informed of what is going forward is extremely important. It develops support, involves others who are interested, and helps to avoid the distrust and other mischief caused by misinformation. It is often the uninvolved who are the conservative and apparently inert elements of a community, but who have concerns, and once an alarm is raised, because they have been uninvolved are most difficult to reach. On the other hand, by awakening their concerns early and involving them in the decision-making process, the interested group can make friends of potential enemies.

Regular publication of agenda before meetings, as well as summaries of information reported, proposals, and progress of planning after meetings, will help to build a climate of acceptance. Even though a small proportion of the community read such stories, many more hear favorably that "something is going on." This is an easier task in a small city or town with an indigenous newspaper. In an urban school setting a group may seek out the neighborhood newspaper, particularly the ethnic papers, ask for space in the school newsletter (or initiate one of its own), and use community agency bulletin boards and other available devices.

The group should respond to school initiatives, even though school personnel as well as community people are involved in the discussions. That is, the group should take into account school action which may have been stimulated by the group's initiative, and con-

---

[33]See Chapter Eight and Appendix for details of the decision-making process.

sider whether the solution is adequate or whether it should be absorbed into a continuing discussion. The issue is not jurisdictional; the objective is not to "win" with a community program over a school program. Rather, the group response should be to welcome, assess, support, and either accept or seek to modify as needed the new administrative action.

For their part, school administrators will find that the partnership procedures outlined here and more fully in the next chapter carry their own safeguards. Such procedures avoid the trap posed by any single strong individual or group bringing ready-made proposals to a community forum, and perhaps making impossible an adequate consideration of needs and issues. Such procedures avoid the win-lose, adversary feelings and jurisdictional conflicts which arise between public and quasi-public groups given overlapping and undefinable powers.Rather, the reality testing of any proposals in an open-membership, lay-professional group provides school boards and school administrators with ample consideration of common problems and ample screening of recommendations for wisdom and feasibility.

The same open membership prevents suppression of innovation on the one hand, and unreasonable proposals on the other, but rather invites both lay and professional participation in a climate productive for education. The trust inherent in partnerships is based in large part on willingness to address fundamental issues, of concern to more than one individual or one group, and on a continuing concern for common objectives. The significant difference between the policy of conflict and the policy of open partnership is that, whereas a policy of conflict tends to seek immediate action to meet the needs of the strongest or loudest, a policy of partnership raises the issues but takes time to enable people to reach understanding.

THE PARTNERSHIP CLIMATE
The ad hoc group dissolves when its purposes have been achieved, but a model and a climate have been established. Left behind are a number of lay and professional individuals who have learned how

people of differing views can work together for common objectives, who have gained the confidence to raise difficult issues and competence in handling them constructively, and who have learned a sense of equality and significance in the community.

The same group may not come together again, but the successful conclusions of one ad hoc group will enable others to organize more easily around another set of problems. Lay-professional and school-community relationships will be noticeably easier.

All of this will have perceptibly good effect on the learning climate of the schools. The Kettering Foundation–supported research in the California schools cited earlier (page 84) drew a pertinent comparison. One of the eight schools studied suffered severe educational problems as well as poor school-community relations. The community people, in fact, had lost confidence in this school because of what they felt was a serious difference in value systems. Research showed that teachers and parents actually held very similar values, but because of lack of communication both groups thought there were hopelessly serious differences. In other schools of the research group, on the other hand, values did differ markedly between parents and teachers; but open and friendly communication between school and community coincided with healthy educational growth in the schools.[34]

The same research project also compared the teachers' evaluation of their principals in these eight schools. It was found that the qualities which support collaboration—tolerance of uncertainty, freedom, and concern for needs and expectations of colleagues—plus initiative for leadership, were ascribed by the teachers to the principals whose schools rated highly for educational effectiveness.[35]

The perceptible improvement in climate does not mean that the benefits of partnership will have been permanently acquired. A

[34]Richard C. Williams, Charles C. Wall, W. Michael Martin, and Arthur Berchin, *Effecting Organizational Renewal in Schools: A Social Systems Perspective*, McGraw-Hill, New York, 1974, pp. 106.

[35]Ibid., p. 26.

school board is likely to have gained respect for citizen action. Its decision-making process may become more collaborative. Administrators are likely to move toward a perception that orchestration of responsibilities is perhaps as effective as personal controls, and perhaps more fruitful.

At the same time, the decisions which have been successfully concluded, and the recommendations which have been officially adopted, must still be monitored for implementation. The work can still be lost if those who are concerned do not follow point to point the successive implementing decisions.

Regular community involvement in a wide variety of ways will continue to be the best safeguard against isolation or apathy in a school system, or against irregularities or dissension. In colloquial terms, community involvement "keeps the system honest," more important, attentive. It facilitates accounting for educational effort in the best sense, in that community people who are closely involved with schools in mutually accepted ways tend to the view that all of us are accountable for what we do. What schools accomplish or do not accomplish comes to be regarded as a shared responsibility.

It is likely that for some time to come community people must take partnership initiatives more often than not, if partnership is to be established. By doing so, they will hasten general recognition that both school administration and community have a high stake in developing an open partnership: a much-needed success in education. To achieve partnership it will be necessary for professional people to accept in their hearts that the school is not a professional preserve, that the school is more than nominally the deep concern of the community, and that the help of the community is actually essential to educational growth; for concerned parents to overcome diffidence and distrust and to accept school faculty and administration as sincerely interested in their children; for nonparent citizens to understand the fundamental stake of society in education for self-renewal, and to accept the need for their own participation; and for all of these to accept the student as partner.

CHAPTER EIGHT

Summary:
To Build a Partnership

A PARTNERSHIP IS a dynamic, never a static, relationship. It is developmental. As we have seen, it can begin very simply, with the gathering of a few people to discuss a common concern, who then reach out to include others; or with the request to an administrator about a problem; "Can we talk about it?" Or, it can begin with an administrator's question, "What do you think about this? Let's talk about it."

One begins with the basic recognition that administrators, teachers, students, parents, and other community members all have a stake in their schools and can best decide together what education programs shall serve their community. People begin with a common concern, not necessarily with the same objectives.

Of the several distinguishing characteristics of the open partnership, *open membership* is primary. The partnership is an educative process, through interaction, through gaining and sharing of new knowledge, and through the effort involved in finding solutions to common problems. Inevitably in the process all members will have developed as individuals by the time decision is arrived at. Since change in institutions depends on change in individuals, it is important that all who will be affected by the decisions involved have opportunity to share in making them, if change is to be effective. If

[158]

there is any question about a membership policy, the test is, Does it result in *inclusion*, not exclusion?

Equal membership is an essential characteristic which grows out of openness in membership and agenda. People may come together with a conscious intent to listen and pay respect to all views, but it is in the process of working together that people come to appreciate each other's different perspectives and knowledge. Members of the group develop a common concern for each other's social and human needs for understanding and mutual cooperation. Thus equal membership is *learned*, and in turn produces a climate of *trust* that is characteristic of successful collaboration. While it is only just to involve individuals in the decisions which affect their lives, the involvement in such decisions on a basis of equality also enhances their self-esteem. The enhancement of self-esteem helps to bring about productive change, and also has a corollary effect in improving the quality of their lives, and thus their social behavior.

Every group comprises many talents, and an outstanding characteristic of partnership is *multiple leadership*—leadership which emerges from the group as occasion requires. A chairman or convener may be elected, or may be named by a group which issues an initial invitation; or perhaps conveners may serve in rotation. But the official leader or convener need not feel sole responsibility to provide direction or information, or even group support. In an open situation these tasks are shared, and the efforts of the group are thereby multiplied.

Probably the most important characteristic of partnership conveners is the kind of openness which encourages others to come forward in different kinds of leadership. People can be counted upon to take a lead in the discussion or in the fact-finding or in analysis in different ways at different times, no matter what their roles may be at other times. Those who raise questions which move the discussion forward, who bring new information, who summarize at appropriate moments, who take a lead in writing position statements for general consideration, who check proposed criteria and proposed solutions: all of these are important leaders.

Conveners, like other leaders, find that the relationship between task orientation and people orientation is best when flexible; leaders lean to one or the other according to the mood and concerns of the group. In general, a greater interest in the task to be performed is more successful when problems are few and people are desirous of moving forward. A greater concern for individuals and their relationships than for the task is helpful when the group appears to be feeling stress.

It is important that all agenda be open, that all members feel able to raise their concerns expecting to be heard objectively, and that all views become part of the total assessment of the matter in hand. At the same time, there is no group pressure to participate. People are expected to contribute according to their concerns and ideas. Only thus can commitment to the process be expected of each member. Given the feeling of commitment among one's colleagues, confidence in the outcome follows.

In the end, every partnership must be tested by the reality of shared decision making. Every collaboration may be said to be in the process of "becoming"; that is, it is developmental. Its objectives may need periodic reassessment. People may agree on limited objectives. Nevertheless, for whatever objectives are undertaken, all the ground work, all the successive steps leading to final decision should be broadly and fully shared. As collaboration grows, and a favorable climate is established, the agenda may broaden; it may eventually include a total educational program, including curricular, fiscal, and staffing decisions.

THE PROCESS

As with most human enterprises, collaboration prospers with the use of certain basic skills. For example, there is inevitably a wide difference in vocabulary within almost any group, let alone in their assumptions about various elements in the complex world of education. Techniques of value clarification help members to arrive at an understanding of one another's ideas with less pain than is sometimes the case. As they move into assessment of the situation and consideration of alternatives these skills become even more important. As with any skill, these are increased by practice. Interested individuals or a group that is seeking to develop collaboration may profit from use of a variety of exercises; examples of these may be found in the appendix on pages 173–177.

The process of finding a solution to a problem follows a fairly well defined pattern, whether it is the main work of an ad hoc group working in collaboration, or the initial effort of a lasting partnership. Care at certain points may determine whether the group will encounter frustration and defeat or arrive at a successful conclusion.

As we have seen, the first meeting should be publicly announced with an open invitation to all persons who may be interested in the subject. It is then important to enable all members to begin the first meeting with an opportunity to identify themselves and their reasons for involvement. The group proceeds to a canvassing of views in an unhurried fashion in order to clarify the common purpose. Too much haste at this point can cripple the partnership.

It is important to take time for an exploration of goals, values, and assumptions about education, teaching, learning, and curriculum. There will be a clarifying of different understandings of meanings of the same words, and common meanings discovered in different vocabularies. Sitting around a table together is a step to partnership, but by itself it is not enough. Hearing what another has to say is necessary, but again by itself it is not enough. It is necessary to respond and to offer further ideas, to reply to the points raised and to seek common ground—not compromise, but ideas that lead to a broader solution that meets common interests. As Paul the Apostle wrote to the Colossians, "Let your speech be always with grace, seasoned with salt, that you may know how to answer each other."[1] Out of these discussions comes a tentative assessment of the situation and perhaps a tentative agreement on the needs of the situation. Integration of the group has begun.

When the area of interest has been tentatively defined, the group again considers who else should be involved. The members develop

[1]Colossians 4:6.

a plan to identify and involve others who may be concerned or affected. One method is to draw a chart of all who could be affected by or could influence implementation of the outcome,[2] and see that invitations are directed to these individuals and groups. They would logically include school board members and administrators who are not already present, as well as municipal officers, the business and religious communities, social agencies, and many others who may be affected. In any case, a continuing open invitation is clearly established and published, with the understanding that the group will reopen any discussion as desired in order to integrate new membership into the developmental thinking. Time that may seem to be lost in this process is actually well spent in ensuring agreements later.

The next stage is fact-finding, in which the total group should be involved. Accurate and adequate information is an essential base for any useful action. Organization into task forces is useful, with parents, teachers, students, and others in each group. The simple plan illustrated in Figure 2 is one possibility.

FIGURE 2

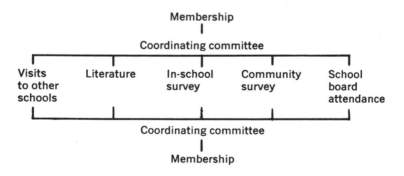

Such questions may be explored as, to what extent is the school system meeting the problem? What is the school system doing to meet the concern? What are other school systems doing or proposing to do? Thorough research on the problems in hand helps to prevent

[2] Appendix, p. 179.

premature and thus unsuccessful decisions. It is important to secure accurate and verifiable information, and best to avoid using confidential information. Such information is impossible to share without sacrificing confidentiality; it is difficult to verify; and its use may well cause personal difficulties. If people are thereby alienated, the enterprise is endangered.

As the group receives information from the task forces, they join in evaluating it for their needs, and then turn to defining the central problem in the light of information now before them. This may be a "risk" period in terms of emotion and possible confrontations, so that the collaborative skills of concern for other people's interests and ingenuity in finding acceptable alternative statements are of crucial value.

Once the problem is defined, the next task is to collect an array of possible alternative solutions. These are screened against the originally defined need. Not yet, however, are possible choices assessed in terms of final solutions, but rather in terms of acceptable *elements* which may be integrated into an acceptable solution. This is another risk period during which patience and collaborative skills are particularly needed.

The final solution is best approached through a series of statements, in which each agreement becomes the basis for more fully developed agreements, so that the final decision is arrived at through a series of successive approximations. It is during this period that the long building of colleagueship and patient reality testing will prove their value in the group's ability to arrive at recommendations or other decisions acceptable to all members.

Now at last, when success has been attained, it is important that the group not close off too quickly.[3] There has been a significant emotional investment which must be respected, for the mental health both of the group and of the community. Plans should be made,

---

[3]Cf. Ralph G. Hirschowitz, M.B., Ch.B., *Small Group Methods in the Promotion of Change within Interagency Networks: Leadership Models*, Laboratory of Community Psychiatry, Harvard Medical School, Boston, Mar. 31, 1971. (Mimeographed.)

perhaps for evaluating the implementation to follow, or for continuing the group on other concerns, or simply for a retrospect of the
activity that has just been concluded. The accomplishment of satisfactory shared decision making not only epitomizes the partnership
upon which the community has embarked; it is a benchmark to which
people can return. It is a tangible, beneficent source of trust in the
general climate.

The full group decision-making process will not be used for all
problems, or on all occasions in which a recommendation is made,
because some decisions can be based on agreements previously arrived at and on continuing consultation with those concerned. But
the group gains immeasurable strength from having learned these
skills, and from knowledge of its ability to arrive successfully at
shared decisions.

With open membership and open agenda, the continuing
partnership is likely to be fluid in composition. It serves as a means
to bring together all who are concerned at any point in the development of the educational program for continued shared decision making; various models of how this develops in practice have been
described in earlier chapters.

A partnership can, like all living organisms, have a life growth
pattern of adolescence, maturity, and perhaps postmaturity. Or, with
continuing openness, it can renew itself. In these terms the partnership serves as a catalyst for educational growth, and at the same
time as a strong support for those entrusted with legal responsibility
for schools—with the proviso that no partnership group ever seeks
control, which is destructive, but maintains the partnership with the
openness which is the source of its strength.

SIGNPOSTS AND CAVEATS

It may be helpful to respond to questions which are sometimes raised
about collaboration. Of all deterrents to partnership the foremost is
probably the ban on disagreement which is the hallmark of hierarchy.
It is all too well known that teachers commonly lose jobs, or prefer-

ment if they are tenured, parents are made clearly unwelcome, and students become objects of hostility, if they are heard to be critical of administrative arrangements. This happens not only in schools but in many agencies and organizations governed on the hierarchic model.

The solution begins with the initial nonthreatening invitation: "Can we talk about it?" Then the discussion moves forward only as all members are comfortable with it, even though apparent progress may be slow in the beginning. Administrators must necessarily be involved in some manner to ameliorate the threatened feelings characteristic of hierarchic leadership. Administrators are commonly attracted by the partnership idea as they learn that partnership does not change their role responsibilities or their role prerogatives, while at the same time they find that benefits do flow from a protocol based on multiple contribution and tolerance of differing opinions. Over a period of time, varying according to the individual, administrators tend to recognize that the line-of-command control is somewhat tenuous in any case in an open system, and contributes to the dysfunction of school management which plagues so many school systems. On the other hand, a colleagueship which is mutually supportive begins to appear more productive and therefore attractive. When the common objective is more effective education, the administrator finds that his own position is enhanced by successful collaboration.

Second among common pitfalls may be the expectation of instant collaboration. Too many people feel that one meeting will serve the purpose. Rather, a single meeting is more likely to be frustrating in its outcomes, for it half opens doors to an exchange of ideas which is never realized. The members of the meeting will not have fully expressed themselves nor will they have properly heard their companions; and if they have not heard others' opinions they will not have explored their own views nor dealt justly with either.

It is a common failing in education that a single exchange of views is accepted as adequate where developmental collaboration is required to arrive at lasting solutions. People may feel the pressure of events for quick decisions, but the outcome all too frequently is a set of decisions that must be reconsidered at another time. When people feel that some sort of time limit must be met, the likelihood is that by a change of pace and a different perspective discussions may be reordered with temporary measures to allow for continuing long-range considerations.

A third deterrent is the feeling of professionalism on the one hand and of "lay ignorance" on the other. Some professional people dislike or at least show restraint in expressing their actual views in a mixed meeting, and yet honest expression of all members is essential to a successful collaboration. In the writer's experience, a useful method for the period of identifying areas of concern is to discuss "druthers"—what could be, rather than what is. The framework of present rules in most schools is inhibiting rather than encouraging to discussion of change, whereas "shaking loose the dreams" encourages warmth and colleagueship and thus more open discussion.

A related deterrent to dialogue is the sometime feeling that decisions must be made by the "knowledgeable." It may be suggested that knowledgeable is a relative term. As Perrone and Strandberg pointed out in regard to parents,[4] nonprofessionals frequently have a "common sense" grasp of educational matters. Many improvements in education have been initiated by laymen, in areas such as special education, school volunteers, and vocational education. Even so, different people are knowledgeable about different matters. Their responsibility is not to claim decision making but to share their information, so that final decisions are made with both information and perspective. Moreover, knowledgeability is enhanced by understanding the possible effects of decisions on others not immediately involved. In collaboration this understanding is a key to the viability of any final decision, and can best be taken into account through sharing an examination of facts on every issue so that the consequences of a variety of decisions are clear.

There is the additional benefit that even the most knowledgeable can gain information from lay views of problems, as well as the

---

[4] Vito Perrone and Warren Strandberg, "A Perspective on Accountability," *Teachers College Record*, February 1972, p. 348.

greater understanding that any of us gains through explaining one's own views and proposals to others. Given the importance of both lay and professional views to the outcomes of educational decision making, there is every reason for equality in their membership.

A fourth deterrent is the expectation that members come with common goals in addressing a common concern. The prime consideration is the common concern: that is, the simple fact that all concerned in a given matter will be affected by the final decision. In such a case the discussion will be devoted to clarification of values until the values and interests specifically pertaining to the matter in hand are satisfactorily distinguished from other differences in views which do not pertain.

For instance, an illustration in an earlier chapter cited a tacit agreement that "We'll try to get together because we both want what's good for kids." It may be that all people whose interests are involved in a school matter are not equally concerned with "what's good for kids." Before the group can go forward with what will serve students and their schools, other interests must be surfaced and respected. One example appeared in the advisory committee which produced the Expanded Curriculum Program described in the second chapter. Some members of the group were chiefly concerned that students were not to be "downtown doing nothing." This question was respected and discussed, and an agreement on it was reached within the first two or three months of the meetings. It is extremely important that such action be taken, as hidden agenda inevitably disserves both collaboration and the viability of final decisions.

A related deterrent is found in the vocabulary differences which occur within any group, not so much because of differences in educational attainment as because of differences in word associations. For instance, educators hear "discrete" as meaning "separate" or "distinct;" the layman hears a different word, "discreet," and thinks "tactful" or "cautious." On one occasion a young man waited until the end of a long committee meeting to ask his neighbor the meaning of the word "dialogue." Another meeting was severely handicapped in its use of time because an educator used "K–12" without mentioning grade levels and some laymen present associated the phrase with "K–9" or "canine" and were understandably bewildered. In such cases people stop listening while they try to "make connection."

For understanding each other's views and each other's vocabulary, therefore, virtually the first question in undertaking a partnership discussion is "Who are we? Why are we here?" It deserves to be explored with a sense of leisure, until people feel sufficiently comfortable with one another to deal openly with their honest concerns.

A fifth question is whether all decisions should be made through collaboration. Obviously there are many decisions which implement accrued policy decisions or commitments previously taken. Random examples would include whether a storm warrants closing the schools or how the press shall be informed about a school "incident." But decisions in which others wish to be involved, such as new curriculum, status of parent volunteers, or the kind of infraction of rules which warrants student suspension, should be shared by those concerned.

A sixth and sometimes major deterrent is the individual who is closely concerned with an issue and will not negotiate, who steadfastly insists upon a course which excludes others who are also deeply concerned and affected. In such a situation a distinction should be found between the individual who may be exerting a territorial imperative, and the issue, which may be difficult to negotiate.

The partnership group would take into account the views of such an individual or minority group, as it would those of any dissidents, and may find that some important interest has been overlooked. It may also be possible that there are some issues the group cannot negotiate. If so, the group can live with the disagreement and work on other issues until the situation and the individuals involved are better known. In the meantime, new perspectives may soften the issue and a means of accommodation may be found. Or, members of the partnership group can investigate the disputed questions for basic principles involved, background history, and possible solutions.

Occasionally the problem is that an individual in a position of significant influence, possibly in a "gatekeeper" position, has indeed asserted territorial prerogative and categorically refuses collaboration. In such a case the group has alternative choices of moving within a more restricted area until some fortuitous development changes the situation, or of working past the obstacle very much as a river flows around a rock in the stream bed. There is seldom a situation in which all directions can be closed off. If time presses, it may be appropriate for the group to reassess its goals and resources and possibly revise its plans, rather than run the risk of foundering on the "rock." The very stimulus of the circumstances and the process of reexamination will itself strengthen the partnership.

The final caveat has to do with power and with equality. A group which has worked through the partnership process and seen its ability to bring about change knows the feeling of power. Its euphoria has been well earned. Individual members have a right to enjoy their feeling of colleagueship. It is important that they not forget, however, that it was colleagueship—their equal membership—more than prowess which earned the group their undeniable but also fleeting moment of power.

If such a group, or some members of it, should seek to bring about other change through the influence which the group has obtained, without going through the same process of involving those who are affected, the group will soon find it has lost its constituency. In losing its constituency, it has also lost its power.

Lasting power lies in equality, but equality comes from working together. Only when people join together in an open partnership to meet a common concern can they be reasonably certain of attaining their objectives.

APPENDIX

1. Open invitation to meet on an identified concern.
2. To set the climate, start from where we are:
   Who are we?
   Why are we here?
3. Sharing views—clarification of purpose:
   Exploration of goals, values, and assumptions about education, teaching, learning, curriculum, etc.
   Clearing of vocabulary and definitions for meanings understandable to one another
   Tentative assessment of situation and needs
   Beginning of integration of the group
4. Who else should be here?
   Develop a plan for identifying and involving others who may be concerned. Analysis of possibly influential people in the area of interest may help to identify others whose views should be involved in discussion.
   Establish an ongoing open invitation and determine how it is to be implemented.
   Plan for review and overlap of discussions for late entrants; emphasize importance of their participation.
5. Fact-finding:
   Total group should be involved. Task force organization is useful.
   Thorough research about a problem helps to avoid premature solutions.
   For example: To what extent is school system meeting the concern? What is the school system doing to meet the concern? What are other school systems doing or proposing to do?

Evaluate information for accuracy, pertinence, credibility, newness, availability.

Define problem in light of information: this is a *risk point* and collaborative skills are important, e.g., continuing recognition and concern for individuals, ingenuity in finding acceptable alternative statements.

6. Assessment of possible solutions:

Collect possible alternative solutions and screen them against needs as originally defined.

Reevaluate needs in light of subsequent information.

Identify *elements* of possible acceptable solutions for *integration* into final solution; this is another *risk point* where patience and collaborative skills are important.

7. Final choices: here is where the long building of colleagueship and value exploration should pay off in smooth decision making and writing of final plans.

8. Phase-out: important for emotional health after long sustained effort. Make plans for follow-up of implementation and evaluation of chosen solution.

Experience suggests:

It is important not to hurry. Avoid letting pressures affect the process; rather, let it develop organically. Recognition of all views will keep it moving. Patience in helping people work through their problems and questions will pay off in reasonable decision making. Organize to meet time pressures, without allowing such pressures to bring about premature decision. That is, arrange a postponement of a time deadline, or take a temporary measure, or a carefully limited measure, to avoid a final decision until appropriate.

Tension:

- Is sometimes useful in maintaining search for agreement.
- Sometimes needs reduction for the moment in order to allow discussion to continue.
- Should not be allowed to bury problems that may hinder final solution.
- Should not be allowed to create pressure for premature decisions.
- Can be reduced by substituting statement-writing for confrontation: try writing statements in pairs or small groups, then take to larger groups.
- May be developed by exploration of personal feelings; this is not useful, as it tends to develop lower rather than higher motivation, but leaders must be aware of, respect, and deal with individual feelings. A partnership group is not a therapy group, but a means of achieving common objectives. If feelings rise, something is being left out or passed over. Try a "round robin" or census-taking to review issues,

objectives, or information still required.

Decisions are accomplished step by step:

- Points to be resolved are distinguished and taken in order, as that order is seen at any given point in the discussions.
- Proposals are superimposed on previous agreements or proposals, as ideas and agreements grow in successive approximations of the final decision.
- Reality testing against previous or known disagreements is important for subsequent acceptance of group decisions.
- Final decision should be acceptable to all members as fully explored and most satisfactory of possible solutions.
- Unwillingness to come to an action decision sometimes occurs. Check to be sure a variety of interest is represented; a mixed group is the best preventive of inaction.

Action Planning May Be Described in Different Vocabularies:

1. Problem identification
   Analysis
   Brainstorming solutions
   Designing concrete plans
   Trying out
2. Problem solving
   Diagnosis
   Generation of alternatives
   Selection
   Action planning
   Taking action
   Evaluation
   Follow-up
3. What?
   So what?
   Now what?

WHAT DO WE ALL THINK? DO WE UNDERSTAND EACH OTHER?

Clarification of goals and assumptions is a natural and essential step early in the development of a partnership. It is not required that people agree in all their values, but that when ideas are discussed the members of a group understand each other. People frequently assign different meanings to the same word, and think of the same concept in terms of different implications. Words which are commonplace to one person may carry strong emotional implications to another. Common goals can be arrived at when the members find acceptable words and phrases on whose meaning they can agree to express the common interest.

The process in which such agreements are arrived at is also an exploration of ideas, in which people gain a better understanding of the problem they are concerned with; at the same time they get to know each other with understanding and respect.

Agree-disagree statements are useful in introducing values discussions in an objective manner and in taking a discussion quickly into some depth without developing confrontation. Some examples which have proved useful to lay, professional, and mixed groups are offered in the following pages. The objective is to find both mutually acceptable concepts and mutually acceptable language in which to express the concept involved.

Rewriting a statement in terms on which a group can agree becomes a useful technique for each step in decision making as leaders or committees write their perceptions into statements about the problems in hand.

Agree-Disagree Statements on Common School-Community Issues

The task is to agree or disagree with each statement, as a group. If the group cannot reach agreement or disagreement, the wording in any statement may be changed enough to allow agreement.

KEY: "A" if you agree—"D" if you disagree

( ) 1. Schools are generally becoming more open to the community, but community pressures have almost invariably forced school doors open.

( ) 2. Those who would change education have to reckon with what the public thinks are the goals of education.

( ) 3. Teachers are authority figures representing management rather than advocates for the student.

( ) 4. Parents and teachers have separate concerns and must avoid possible conflict.

( ) 5. School-community groups must avoid questions of special interest in order to arrive at viable solutions.

Agree-Disagree Statements on Common School Governance Issues

The task is to agree or disagree with each statement, as a group. If you cannot reach agreement or disagreement, you may change the wording in any statement enough to allow agreement.

KEY: "A" if you agree—"D" if you disagree

( ) 1. School boards cannot share responsibilities for which decision is legally theirs.
( ) 2. Alternative institutions offer no threat to existing institutions.
( ) 3. Staff-community conflicts are mirrored in student behavior.
( ) 4. School staff can support and strengthen family roles in the education and development of their students.
( ) 5. Relationships between administrators and parents can improve the democratic climate of the school.
( ) 6. Fiscal support of schools depends largely on collective public confidence.
( ) 7. School operation is inhibited as much by fears of what the community will say as it is by actual disapproval.

Agree-Disagree Statements about Partnerships

The task is to agree or disagree with each statement, as a group. If the group cannot reach agreement or disagreement, the wording in any statement may be changed enough to allow agreement.

KEY: "A" if you agree—"D" if you disagree

( ) 1. The board of education must assume leadership in any plan to involve citizens at the local level in educational planning.
( ) 2. Initiative for programs in community-school partnerships must be in the hands of a nonprofessional community member.
( ) 3. One test of real community involvement is the degree of control the community has over curriculum.
( ) 4. Teachers must have a final approval of programs developed by school and community groups.
( ) 5. Bilingual programs should be instituted even though the population of those in the school who speak the second language is very small.
( ) 6. Representatives of industry, city government, health, and higher education should be selected by the principal in establishing a partnership arrangement.
( ) 7. An advisory board to the school board can begin the process of a partnership.
( ) 8. Results of real partnership arrangements are (a) parents as teacher aides; (b) student visits to local businesses; (c) teacher-parent conferences.

The exploration of individual roles may help group members sort out their views of relationships among various partners.

School-Community Partnership Roles

Make individual choices first—then discuss as a group. Identify both agreements and points at issue.

1. School-community partnership groups:
   (a) Must serve established school goals.
   (b) Can develop new goals.
   (c) Can explore new educational ground.
   (d) Should be limited to accepted interests.
2. School boards fulfill their legal responsibilities:
   (a) By controlling decisions on all substantive issues.
   (b) By deciding only broad policy issues.
   (c) By reviewing for policy approval decisions taken at other levels, e.g., by principals, teachers, etc.
   (d) By accepting recommendations of broadly representative school-community groups.
   (e) By involving those affected or concerned in considerations leading to policy decisions.
3. Superintendents:
   (a) Are responsible for fulfilling school board policies.
   (b) Are responsible for separating policy issues from administrative issues.
   (c) Should protect school administration prerogatives if, for instance, actions of principals differ with views of school board members.
   (d) Should take leadership in school-community collaboration.
   (e) May use collaboration to address own problems.
   (f) Should allow school-community groups to develop leadership.
   (g) Should accept/guard against development of *ad hoc* interest groups.
   (h) Are wise/unwise in making open invitations for expression of individual interests.
4. Teachers:
   (a) Are wholly responsible for classroom curriculum.
   (b) Can profitably discuss curriculum with each other/parents.
   (c) Share responsibility for curriculum with administration/school board/community.
   (d) Can utilize school-community collaboration to develop/improve curriculum.
5. Partnership:
   (a) Can exist within the school community, i.e., between board and superintendent, administration and teachers, etc.

(b) Can have little/significant effect on school support/curriculum.

(c) Must be based on legal or quasi-legal authorization.

(d) Can be developed on an ad hoc basis, i.e., involving any concern of any group.

6. Partnership begins:

(a) With people of like interests.

(b) With willingness to share other people's concerns.

(c) With interest in finding people with like concerns.

(d) With a felt need about the school.

(e) With willingness of people with different interests to talk together.

(f) When mutual respect and trust are established.

7. Partnership requires (rank your choices):

(a) Voluntary/directed participation of school people, community people, and students.

(b) Organization.

(c) Equal willingness to contribute

(d) Surfacing of individual interests.

(e) Honest exchange of views.

(f) Willingness to continue discussions.

(g) Skills in listening, compromise, and consensus.

(h) Sense of reality.

(i) Willingness to act.

(j) Respect between members.

8. Partnership is successful when (rank your choices):

(a) Outcome meets initial expectations.

(b) School people and community people have learned to talk with each other.

(c) Community support of schools is increased.

(d) The level of trust is significantly raised.

(e) Participants feel education is improved.

Suggestions about Group Decision Making

Group decision making is a process for making full use of available resources and for utilizing different views creatively. Complete unanimity is not the goal, and is rarely achieved. On the other hand, a group decision should be acceptable to every member as logical, desirable, and feasible. This means that a single person can block the group if he or she believes it necessary—an option which should be used in the interests of the common objectives. The following suggestions help in achieving agreement.

1. Avoid arguing for your own proposals. Present your position as lucidly and logically as possible, but listen to the reactions of others and consider these carefully before pressing a point.

2. Do not assume that one must win and another must lose when discussion reaches a stalemate. Instead, look for the next most acceptable alternative for all parties.

3. Do not change your mind simply to avoid conflict and to reach agreement and harmony. When agreement seems to come too quickly and easily, one should be suspicious. Explore the reasons and be sure that all members accept the solution for basically similar or compatible reasons. Yield only to positions that have objective and logically sound bases.

4. Avoid conflict-reducing techniques such as majority vote, averages, flipping a coin, or bargaining. When a dissenting member finally agrees, there is no reason to feel that he or she must be rewarded by "winning" on some later point.

5. Differences of opinion are natural and helpful. Seek them out and try to involve everyone in the decision process. Disagreements can help the group come to a decision because with a wide range of information and opinion, there is a better chance that the group will hit upon more adequate solutions.

WORKSHEET

This is the problem, as we see it:

_____

_____

_____

_____

_____

_____

_____

_____

_____

This is what we want to happen:
(List objectives in order of importance.)

1. _____

_____

2. _____

_____

3. _____

_____

Who is concerned with our problem?

Probably *for* our objectives   May be *against* our objectives

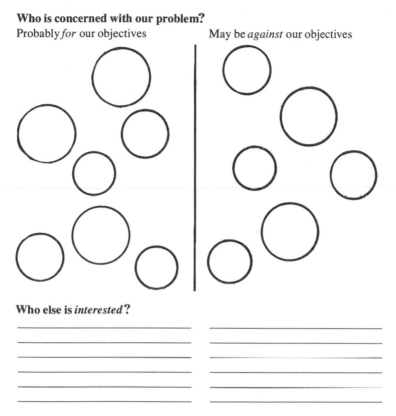

Who else is *interested*?

_____	_____
_____	_____
_____	_____
_____	_____
_____	_____

Draw lines between those who influence each other to begin charting a partnership network.

What do we need to know?

List needed information as it occurs to you: Task group
                                                                number

_____	_____
_____	_____
_____	_____
_____	_____
_____	_____
_____	_____
_____	_____
_____	_____

Divide above items into task groups. List title for each group and assign task group number to each item.

(1) _____

(2) _____

(3) _____

(4) _____

INTERVIEW RECORD SHEET

What did I/we hear _____ I/we judge this to be:

say about _____ :

	FACT	ATTI-TUDE	BE-LIEF	INTER-EST
1. Q.				
A.				
2. Q.				
A.				
3. Q.				
A.				
4. Q.				
A.				
5. Q.				
A.				
6. Q.				
A.				
7. Q.				
A.				

Interviewer(s)

Source: Roland Goddu.

FACT COLLECTION SHEET

What *facts* do we know about _____ :

FACT	SOURCE	DATE	COLLECTOR

WORKSHEET: FORCE FIELD ANALYSIS

Immediate goal: _____

Helping forces	*Hindering forces*
1.	1.
2.	2.
3.	3.
4.	4.
5.	5.
6.	6.

List helping and hindering forces.

Note whether some helping forces may be matched to remove or weaken some hindering forces.

Note how helping forces may be strengthened.

Note how remaining hindering forces may be countered or weakened, by such means as better information, involvement in activity, etc.

Develop plans for indicated action.

LEADERSHIP ROLES

Group Building and Maintenance Roles	1. *Supports, encourages*—attempts to offer warmth and support so that others will feel free to contribute;indicates understanding and acceptance of other points of view, ideas, and suggestions. 2. *Reduces tension*—attempts to reduce tension, when reduction needed, by humor or by steering conversation to safe ground. 3. *Compromises*—when his own idea or status is involved in a conflict offers a compromise which yields status; admits error; modifies in interest of group cohesion. 4. *Initiates*—introduces new ideas or procedures; tries to get movement started toward a goal.
Task Roles	5. *Facilitates introduction of needed information*—tries to communicate needed information; expresses and asks for opinions; reacts to suggestions by others. 6. *Reality tests*—makes a critical analysis of an idea; tests an idea against some data; tries to see if the idea would work. 7. *Clarifies issues*—shows, or clarifies, the relations among various ideas and suggestions and how they relate to the task. 8. *Elaborates*—spells out suggestions in terms of examples to develop meanings; expands and adds to ideas. 9. *Summarizes*—pulls together related ideas; restates suggestions; offers a decision or conclusion for group to consider.
Nonfunctional Roles	10. *Dominates group*—tries to assert authority or superiority by manipulating other persons. 11. *Nitpicks*—tends to magnify insignificant details; overlooks significant aspects because of attention to minor details. 12. *Expresses hostility*—tries to deflate the status of others by expressing disapproval of their values, acts, or feelings.

Source: National PTA Field Service.

ATTITUDES CONSTRUCTIVE TO PARTNERSHIPS

Constructive group relationships grow out of (1) the continuing desire to understand the feelings and communications of another person as they seem to that person at the moment, together with (2) a feeling of freedom to explore. The administrator or leader who creates such a climate in his or her group or organization will find people more self-responsible, more creative, better able to adapt to new problems, more basically cooperative.

The following table was suggested by a reading of Carl Rogers' essay entitled *On Becoming a Person*:[1]

Helping Attitudes	*Nonhelping Attitudes*
Acceptant, democratic	Actively rejectant
Goals oriented to persons	Goals oriented to problems
Emphasis on person-to-person relationships	Emphasis on procedure
Openness of expressing real feelings	Lack of interest
Statements which clarify	Vagueness
Effort to understand colleagues	Remoteness
Respect for independence of choice	Direct specific advice
Focus on present problems	Emphasis on past history
Sensitivity to attitudes	Anxiety
Warm interest without emotional overinvolvement	Excessive sympathy
Mutual liking and respect	Suggestion of threat
Trustworthiness in fulfilling commitment	Judgment

HELPING BEHAVIORS

Individual behavior in a group is likely to vary in different situations; but the more people tend to behaviors that build rather than destroy a group, the more productive a partnership is likely to be.

Destroying Behaviors	*Building Behaviors*
Indoctrinate	Assist
Build oneself	Build others
Work for change for the sake of change	Work to improve present practice
Interfere with decision making	Facilitate decision making

[1]Carl R. Rogers, *On Becoming a Person*, Houghton Mifflin Company, Boston, 1961.

Take public credit for group success	Increase sense of group accomplishment
Depreciate the position of leadership	Show appreciation of challenges faced by group leadership
Block communications with killer phrases, loaded openings, etc. . . .	Facilitate communication by listening, feedback, skillful questioning

Source: Adapted from materials of Project ADAPTA, National Congress of Parents and Teachers and the North Dakota Congress of Parents and Teachers, 1971.

TWO POSSIBLE TIME LINES FOR CARRYING OUT A PROJECT:

	SEPTEMBER	OCTOBER	NOVEMBER	DECEMBER	JANUARY	FEBRUARY	MARCH	APRIL	MAY
1.	Members agree on general priority areas—committee established on *this* priority	Committee begins to define area—starts subcommittees on fact-finding	Subcommittees report—committee refines definition of problem, decides objectives, and reports to members for action	Subcommittees decide what new facts are needed and who else should be involved	Subcommittees continue fact-finding and talks with many groups—feedback reported to committee	Committee organizes facts and develops plan to meet objectives	In several meetings committee develops details of plan in written recommendation	Committee reports detailed program to membership	Plan presented to school board
2.	Members agree on general priority areas—committee established on this priority—committee defines problem, invites all possibly concerned to second meeting which redefines problem and establishes subcommittees	Subcommittees gather facts, report to committee, which decides recommendation on objectives	Committee reports to membership and receives approval for recommended objective—committee allocates implementation tasks	Subcommittees plan their tasks, report to committee, and recheck involvement of all concerned	Implementation begins; public kept informed; subcommittees report	Work continues; progress report to membership and general public	Implementation evaluated—committee gathers data for recommendations to membership	Committee reports to membership—recommends next steps, if any	

BIBLIOGRAPHY

BOOKS

American Association of School Administrators: *School Board-Superintendent Relationships*, Washington, D.C., 1956.

Bendiner, Robert: *The Politics of Schools*, Harper & Row, Publishers, Incorporated, New York, 1969.

Blake, Robert R., and Jane Srygley Mouton: *The Managerial Grid*, Gulf Publishing Company, Houston, 1964.

Campbell, Roald F., Luvern L. Cunningham, and Roderick F. McPhee: *The Organization and Control of American Schools*, Charles E. Merrill Books, Inc., Columbus, Ohio, 1965.

Cook, Paul W., Jr.: *Modernizing School Governance for Educational Equality and Diversity*, Massachusetts Advisory Council on Education, Boston, 1972.

Education for the People: A Resource Book for School-Community Decision Making, Education Resources Center, San Mateo County, Calif., 1971.

Getzels, Jacob W., James M. Lipham, and Roald F. Campbell: *Educational Administration as a Social Process*, Harper & Row, Publishers, Incorporated, New York, 1968.

Hersey, Paul, and Kenneth H. Blanchard: *Management of Organizational Behavior*, Prentice-Hall, Inc., Englewood Cliffs, N.J., 1972.

Institute for Responsive Education: *Together: Schools and Communities*, Massachusetts Advisory Council on Education, Boston, August 1975.

Likert, Rensis: *New Patterns of Management*, McGraw-Hill Book Company, New York, 1961.

McCarty, Donald J., and Charles E. Ramsey: *The School Managers: Power and Conflict in American Public Education*, Greenwood Publishing Corporation, Westport, Conn., 1971.

McGregor, Douglas: *The Human Side of Enterprise*, McGraw-Hill Book Company, New York, 1960.

McPherson, Gertrude H.: *Small Town Teacher*, Harvard University Press, Cambridge, Mass., 1972.

Maslow, Abraham: *Motivation and Personality*, Harper & Brothers, New York, 1954.

May, Rollo: *Power and Innocence*, W. W. Norton & Company, Inc., New York, 1972.

Metcalf, Henry C., and L. Urwick: *Dynamic Administration: The Collected Papers of Mary Parker Follett*, Harper & Brothers, New York, 1940.

National Commission on Resources for Youth: New Roles for Youth in the School and the Community, Citation Press, New York, 1974.

National Committee for Citizens in Education: *Public Testimony on Public Schools*, McCutchan Publishing Corporation, Berkeley, Calif., 1975.

_____: *Violence in Our Schools: What to Know about It—What to Do about It*, Columbia, Md., 1975.

Nolte, M. Chester: *An Introduction to School Administration: Selected Readings*, The Macmillan Company, New York, 1966.

Overstreet, Harry, and Bonaro Overstreet: *Where Children Come First*, National Congress of Parents and Teachers, Chicago, 1949.

Pierson, H. L.: *Shaping the Schools: A Guide to Boardmanship*, 2d ed., Harold L. Pierson, New Hampton, N.H., 1973.

Rogers, Carl R.: *On Becoming a Person*, Houghton Mifflin Company, Boston, 1961.

Rosenthal, Robert, and Lenore Jacobson: *Pygmalion in the Classroom: Teacher Expectation and Pupils' Intellectual Development*, Holt, Rinehart, and Winston, Inc., New York, 1968.

Sterling, Philip: *The Real Teachers*, Random House, Inc., New York, 1972.

Task Force '74, *The Adolescent, Other Citizens, and Their High Schools: A Report to the Public and the Profession*, McGraw-Hill Book Company, New York, 1975.

Thomas, Donald R.: *The Schools Next Time: Explorations in Educational Sociology*, McGraw-Hill Book Company, New York, 1973.

Williams, Richard C., Charles C. Wall, W. Michael Martin, and Arthur Berchin: *Effecting Organizational Renewal in Schools: A Social Systems Perspective*, McGraw-Hill Book Company, New York, 1974.

Zeigler, L. Harmon, and M. Kent Jennings, with G. Wayne Peak, *Governing American Schools: Political Interaction in Local School Districts*, Duxbury Press, North Scituate, Mass., 1974.

Zimet, Melvin: *Decentralization and School Effectiveness*, Teachers College Press, New York, 1973.

ARTICLES, PAPERS, AND REPORTS

Analysis to Reduce Property Damage, Harvard University, Graduate School of Design, Architectural Research Office, Massachusetts Advisory Council on Education, Boston, 1975.

Anson, Ronald J.: "The Educator's Response to *Goss* and *Wood*," *Phi Delta Kappan*, September 1975.

Brophy, Jere E., and Thomas L. Good: "Teacher Expectations: Beyond the Pygmalion Controversy," *Phi Delta Kappan*, December 1972.

Buxton, Thomas H., and Keith W. Prichard: "Student Perceptions of Teacher Violations of Human Rights," *Phi Delta Kappan*, September 1973.

Coleman, James S.: *How Do the Young Become Adults?* paper presented to the American Educational Research Association, Chicago, 1972.

Davies, Don: *Citizen Participation in Education: Annotated Bibliography*, Institute for Responsive Education, New Haven, Conn., 1973.

——: "The Emerging Third Force in Education," *Inequality in Education*, Harvard University, Center for Law and Education, Cambridge, Mass., November 1973.

Dodson, Dan W.: "Authority, Power, and Education," in *Education for an Open Society*, Association for Supervision and Curriculum Development, Washington, D.C., 1974.

Education Commission of the States, *NAEP Newsletter*, Denver, December 1973; January 1974.

Fantini, Mario: Untitled speech to the National Consortium on Educational Alternatives, Nov. 8, 1971, *Changing Schools*, No. 002, Educational Alternatives Project, Indiana University, Bloomington n.d.

Gallup, George H.: "Seventh Annual Gallup Poll of Public Attitudes toward Education," *Phi Delta Kappan*, December 1975.

Gray, Farnum, with Paul S. Graubard and Harry Rosenberg: "Little Brother Is Changing You," *Psychology Today*, March 1974.

Haskins, Kenneth W.: "Implications: New Conceptions of Relevancy," *Educational Leadership*, May 1972.

Hirschowitz, Ralph G., M.B., Ch.B.: *Small Group Methods in the Promotion of Change within Interagency Networks; Leadership Models*, Laboratory of Community Psychiatry, Harvard Medical School, Boston, Mar. 31, 1971. (Mimeographed.)

House, James E.: "Can the Student Participate in His Own Destiny?" *Educational Leadership*, February 1970.

Knickerbocker, Irving: "Leadership: A Conception and Some Implications," *Journal of Social Issues*, Summer 1948.

McPartland, James, et al.: *Student Participation in High School Decisions: A Study of Students and Teachers in Fourteen Urban High Schools, Summary and Excerpts*, Johns Hopkins University, Center for the Study of Social Organization of Schools, Baltimore, 1971.

Mood, Alexander M.: *Do Teachers Make a Difference?* Bureau of Educational Personnel Development, U.S. Office of Education, 1970.

Morgan, Frank W., Jr.: "Vermont's Community-involved 'Open' School," *American Education,* June 1973.

National Congress of Parents and Teachers: *Proceedings*, Chicago, 1964.

_____: *Reports, Committee for Organizational Study*, 1967–1969.

_____: and the North Dakota Congress of Parents and Teachers: *A Tool Kit for Project ADAPTA*, Chicago, 1971.

_____: and Charlotte–Mecklenburg Public Schools, Charlotte, N.C.: *Someone Has to Listen* (film), 1973.

National School Public Relations Association: *Citizens Advisory Committees: Current Trends in School Policies and Programs*, Arlington, Va., 1973.

_____: *Discipline Crisis in Schools: The Problems, Causes, and Search for Solutions*, Arlington, Va., 1973.

_____: *Education U.S.A.*, Jan. 21, Mar. 11, Mar. 25, Apr. 22, 1974, and Jan. 13, 1975.

_____: *It Starts in the Classroom*, Arlington, Va., January 1974, January 1975.

_____: *The School Board Meeting*, Washington, D.C., 1970.

_____: *School Boards in an Era of Conflict, Education U.S.A.* Special Report, Highlights of the Cubberly Conference, Stanford University, Stanford, Calif., July 26–28, Washington, D.C., 1966.

_____: *School Volunteers: Districts Recruit Aides to Meet Rising Costs, Student Needs*, Arlington, Va., 1973.

_____: *TRENDS in School Public Relations*, Washington, D.C., Dec. 15, 1968.

Palmer, Parker, and Elden Jacobsen: *Action Research: A New Style of Politics in Education*, Institute for Responsive Education, Boston, 1974.

Perrone, Vito, and Warren Strandberg: "A Perspective on Accountability," *Teachers College Record*, February 1972.

Pitman, John C.: *Summary of Actions Taken by Selected States Involved in Developing Competency-based Certification Systems*, New England Program in Teacher Education, Durham, N.H., August 1973.

Reimanis, Gunars: *Teaching Effectiveness and the Interaction Between Teaching Methods, Student and Teacher Characteristics*, Corning Community College, Corning, N.Y., 1972.

Rich, Leslie: "The Magic Ingredient of Volunteerism," *American Education*, June 1973.

Shaw, Archibald B., and John Lyon Reid: "The Random Falls Idea: An Educational Program and Plant for Youth and Community Growth," *School Executive*, March 1956.

The Shrewsbury Plan, Shrewsbury, Mass., Public Schools, 1973.

Sizemore, Barbara A.: "Community Power and Education," *Education for an Open Society*, Association for Supervision and Curriculum Development, Washington, D.C., 1974.

Telfer, Richard G.: "Staff Involvement: Key to Curriculum Improvement," *The Clearing House*, May 1969.

USDESEA: *Community Involvement in USDESEA*, Department of the Army, Directorate, United States Dependents Schools, European Area, Pamphlet No. 360-6, September 1975.

Watson, Peter, European Correspondent, report on research of Roy Nash, North Wales University College, in *Behavior Today*, Dec. 17, 1973.

Wednesday, vol. 7, no. 5, Princeton Public Schools, Princeton, N.J., Feb. 6, 1974.

West, Alan M.: "What's Bugging Teachers," *Saturday Review*, Oct. 16, 1965.

Westin, Alan F., and Deann Murphy: *Civic Education in a Crisis Age: An Alternative to Repression and Revolution*, Summary of a Research Project to Develop Objectives for a New Civic Education Curriculum for American Secondary Schools in the 1970s, Columbia University and Teachers College, New York, September 1970.

Wilkinson, Doreen H.: *Community Schools: Education for Change*, National Association of Independent Schools, Boston, November 1973.

Young, Dean A.: "A Legitimate Right . . . Students' Role in Decision Making," *MASC Journal*, Massachusetts Association of School Committees, March 1973.

Youngerman, Stephenson S., Jr.: *The Decentralized Administrative Concept*, A Report to the Board of Trustees, Boise City Independent District, Boise, Idaho, Jan. 3, 1972.

INDEX